Dor Knap
Its History & Toc H Life

"The House on the Hill"

by David Encill, Ray Fabes, George Lee & Lionel Powell

Copyright © 2004 David Encill

Published by Cortex Design – www.cortex-design.co.uk

Reprinted 2020

Incorporating a history of Broadway, the Hill & Tower in Worcestershire and the history of a remarkable house used as a Toc H Conference Centre, 1959—1979.

All proceeds to charity

ISBN-10: 0954919602

ISBN-13: 9780954919603

Photos front cover: the cast-iron sign (top-right) and Dor Knap house, c.1965

Dor Knap, its History & Toc H Life is copyright © 2004, David Encill, Ray Fabes, George Lee, Lionel Powell
All rights reserved.

Published in Great Britain by: Cortex Design
55 Bewell Head, Bromsgrove, Worcestershire. B61 8HX. UK
www.cortex-design.co.uk

Reprinted 2020

Typeset in 10pt. Zapf Humanist

This publication is Copyright © 2004 the authors, except for the rights to the material listed below. No part of this publication may be stored, reproduced or transmitted in any form or by any means, on any media, mechanical or electronic, including photocopying or recording, without the prior written permission of the authors.

1889 Map of Broadway and Dor Knap is Copyright © and/or Database Right Landmark Information Group and Ordnance Survey Crown Copyright and/or Database Right 2002. All rights reserved.
Photo of John Wesley, Copyright © "The Wesley Center Online": http://wesley.nnu.edu
Photo of Broadway Tower, Copyright © 2000 David Scott, www.cubeis.co.uk
Line Drawings, Copyright © Gary Jones
All other rights are respected.

While every care has been taken in the writing and compilation of this book, the publisher and authors cannot accept any liability for the information contained herein.

ISBN 9780954919603

All profit from sales of this book goes to Charity

www.toch-uk.org.uk

Contents

Introduction 7
A History of Broadway, the Hill & Tower 9
Middle Hill Estate & Dor Knap until 1938: Humble Beginnings 12
Dor Knap before Toc H occupation: 1938-1957 14
Dor Knap – Toc H Life: 1959-1979 16
Dor Knap: the 'his' and 'her' story of Toc H 19
The House Itself 20
Regular activities 23
Special Events 26
The Chapel 28
Tales of Dor Knap 30
Painting and Music Week 1979 (Dor Knap – Hail and Farewell) 42
The Wardens 44
The Friends of Dor Knap 46
The Cotswold Festivals 48
1939–1979: How this came to be written in 2004 53
Postscript: Dor Knap today 55
Appendix I: What is Toc H? 56
Appendix II: Artwork 58
Appendix III: Domesday Book 59
Appendix IV: Changing Logos 59
Acknowledgements 60
References 60
Index 61

Introduction

Following an historical account into the magnificent village of Broadway, Broadway Hill and the Tower, this book attempts to capture the unique part played by Dor Knap, the Toc H Conference and Training Centre, during the period 1959-1979. It has been compiled from the reminiscences of many who shared the experiences this special place had to offer them and to the Movement in general.

There was something about Dor Knap that was difficult to define unless one used the word 'magic'; it was an inspiration to many. Some of us still go out of our way, when in the vicinity of Broadway, to take a wistful glance up the drive or look down on the scene from Broadway Tower. The memories come flooding back and we can reflect on the changes in our lives that our Dor Knap experiences created.

This book attempts to capture some of that infectious spirit and to provide a channel through which readers can reflect on the various stages of Dor Knap, its Toc H life.

We acknowledge the contributions of many people, too numerous to mention all by name, who have offered their insights, their photos, their drawings and their poems – we trust our words do justice to the story we seek to convey.

Right: Dor Knap as so many people remember it: mellow ochre-coloured Cotswold stone and grey slates overlooking a scenic landscape.

Left: The sign that greeted visitors

Dor Knap: its History & Toc H Life
"The House on the Hill"

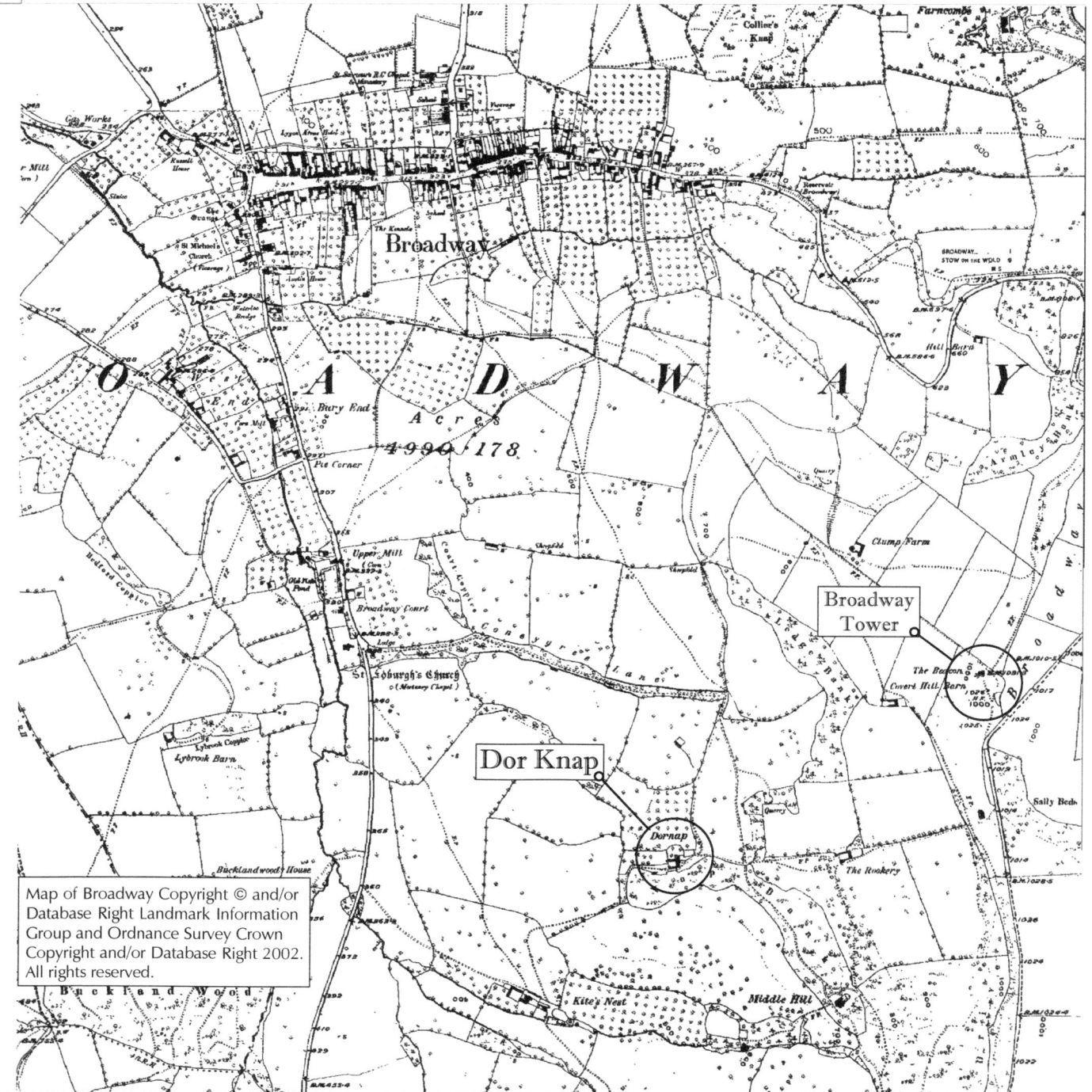

Map of Broadway Copyright © and/or Database Right Landmark Information Group and Ordnance Survey Crown Copyright and/or Database Right 2002. All rights reserved.

A History of Broadway, the Hill & Tower

It would be extremely remiss if we leapt straight into an account of Dor Knap's history without first exploring its environs, in particular the village of Broadway and the tower that dominates the adjoining Beacon Hill.

Broadway

On the northern edge of the picturesque Cotswolds lies the village of Broadway, built exclusively from mellow ochre-coloured Cotswold stone that epitomises everyone's image of a typical English village, and one having a very rich heritage.

Dating to when it was first established as a settlement could be from the Battle of Dyrham when the Saxon invasion was repelled in 557AD, although it came 'on the map' during the Roman occupation when a road was struck past Broadway Hill. With the village being favourably positioned between London and Worcester it naturally became an ideal staging point on this route and further raised its prominence. However, a mention in the Domesday Book in 1086 (see App. III) places no doubt that the village was founded prior to Norman times, when possession of the land in and around the village came to the local Benedictine Abbey of Pershore in 972AD, which lasted until the Reformation of 1538.

According to *Noake's Guide to Worcestershire*, 1868, Henry III (r. 1216-1272) granted Broadway a market and three days fair, while Henry VII (r. 1485–1509) also contributed to Broadway's history when a Royal statute proclaimed that all persons who held land in the manor were compelled to pay one penny annually towards repairing the parish church, St. Eadburgha, or forfeit twenty pence.

At the time of the Reformation during Henry VIII's reign (r. 1509-1547) in 1538, it is rumoured that before the King's Commissioner arrived, the silver mass bells from St. Eadburgha were hidden in the grounds of Dor Knap. While never recovered, apparently they can sometimes be heard ringing on the hillside!

Broadway no doubt derived its modern name because of the very wide main street, which is lined on both sides with a variety of fascinating buildings. In particular the very imposing Lygon Arms hotel is worthy of immediate mention, not least because both protagonists of the English Civil War (1642-1648), Oliver Cromwell and King Charles I, stayed there at different times. The building was originally created from two farmhouses, with the earliest dating from the sixteenth century although this could be even earlier.

Broadway 1971. Note the Tower in the middle distance on top of the Hill. The Swan Inn is on the left and the road leading to Snowshill turns right just in front of the tree

John Wesley, c.1740
© The Wesley Center Online:
www.wesley.nnu.edu

During calmer times, a regular visitor to St. Eadburgha was John Wesley (1703-1791), who would regularly travel from Oxford to preach here. His teachings were to form the basis of the Methodist Church and this religious revival no doubt helped pacify England during darker, more revolutionary times across the rest of Europe.

Towards the end of the main street is the famous Fish Hill that allowed the parish to be enclosed when built in 1771; the new road was made and the Fish Inn (certainly a strange name for a building 1,000 feet above sea level) was erected at the top. Now, turning the calendar forward over two hundred years, Fish Hill has once again been blocked off to relieve Broadway of ever-increasing traffic flow, and access to Broadway is only possible by circumnavigating the hill.

Moving back down to the bottom of the High Street can be found The Green where Church Street bears off to the right. Following this narrow winding road leads to the smaller 'chocolate box' village of Snowshill – also worthy of a visit because of the lavender fields – and about one mile before reaching Snowshill is the driveway that formerly led to Dor Knap: now privately owned, with the emphasis very much on "private"!

Broadway Hill & Tower

Outside the village Broadway (or Beacon) Hill rises to 1,024 feet (312 metres) above sea level and is the second highest point in the Cotswolds. Back in 1660 it gained particular notoriety following the disappearance of a 70-year old rent collector, William Harrison. His manservant duly confessed to the murder, implicated his mother and brother, and all three were subsequently tried and hanged on Broadway Hill, despite no body ever being found. Some two years later Harrison unexpectedly reappeared, claiming to have been kidnapped and taken to Turkey before escaping back to England! This event became known as The Campden Wonder.

Broadway Tower.
Copyright © 2000 David Scott
www.cubeis.co.uk

Notoriety aside, Broadway Hill offers magnificent views across a wide area of the Cotswolds and was an ideal place to build the now famous Tower. This was originally constructed in the late eighteenth century by the 6th Earl of Coventry as a folly: fashionable for the period to demonstrate the landowner's wealth and it could be seen from his family seat in Worcester, some 20 miles away and is now part of an extensive Country Park.

This impressive 65-foot tall structure became the home of many eminent people; the eccentric bibliophile Sir Thomas Phillipps (1792-1872) and owner of Middle Hill Estate, amassed the largest private collection of books and manuscripts in the world, and even had a printing press installed in the Tower until 1862 to produce his own publications. The operation was appropriately called Middle Hill Press.

Another notable resident was William Morris (1834-1896), the artist and interior designer who is credited with founding the Art & Crafts Movement that was most prominent from 1880-1900.

During this time the doors to Broadway Tower greeted various notables, including Morris' artist friends, Edward Burne-Jones (1833-1898) and Dante Gabriel Rossetti (1828-1882) – the latter being leader of the Pre-Raphaelite School that broke away from the conventional form of art. Rossetti was known to have lived at Broadway Tower for a period, during which time he eloped with Morris' wife Janie, scandalising the moralistic Victorian society.

William Morris

The importance of William Morris' work cannot be underestimated. Although he was never widely celebrated as an artist, as a designer he excelled and it his incredibly detailed textile and wallpaper designs in particular that showed his real aptitude.

Heavily influenced by Medieval and Gothic themes, the designs even today, some 120 years later, are still being hand-printed to an incredible degree of accuracy, by craftsman using the original woodblocks.

A humorous pen & ink of Morris by Rossetti

Best known of these manufacturers is Arthur Sanderson & Sons Ltd, who acquired the original woodblocks from the Morris & Company when they ceased trading in 1940, and continue to trade using this name.

An extract from Morris' Honeysuckle design that ably demonstrates the sheer intricacy of his designs

Middle Hill Estate & Dor Knap until 1938: Humble Beginnings

Although historical records of Dor Knap (or Nap) are rather sparse, the name could be associated with a shepherd's croft according to John Callf's 1967 articles, *The Song of Dor Knap*, which was built during the Danish occupation c.500AD. The word 'dor' could possibly refer to a 'pass' with 'nap' meaning 'hill', and a record in the Domesday Book certainly supports the existence of a croft in 1085. John also mentions that during Elizabethan times; 'the road from Worcester to London followed the line of Conygree Lane, which is the first part of the present Dor Knap drive after entering the lodge gates…' Naturally, Dor Knap was soon adopted as "The House on the Hill".

Additionally, to quote exclusively from the original Toc H publicity booklet as written by Alec Churcher, 1959:

> *The Malverns and the Welsh Marches are unforgettable. The house itself, built of mellow Cotswold stone and tiles, has a character of its own and the view over the Vale of Evesham is also unforgettable.*

We are told that the name Dor Knap is Saxon for "little place on the hill" (although some said "under the hill"). In the Domesday Book (A.D. 1085) there is a record of a shepherd's croft approximately on the site on which Dor Knap now stands and it seems reasonably certain that the place was originally a tiny farmhouse consisting of two back rooms and a kitchen with bedrooms and attics above. The present kitchen, dining-room, and small 'library', with the rooms above, are the oldest part of the house and probably date back to Elizabethan times. During the course of its long life many alterations and additions have been made to the original buildings, the last of them – in 1910 – being a pleasantly proportioned music-room or ballroom, which now provides us with a large conference room of almost ideal size for our purpose.

The oak-beamed room with inglenook would appear to confirm it dating back to Elizabethan times, and the small window is probably a relic from the days when glass was far too expensive to be used in ordinary farmhouses, in particular when the unpopular 'Window Tax' (1696) was in force at around this time.

It is known that until recently Dor Knap was part of the Middle Hill Estate, the largest area of land in Broadway where certain buildings were leased to tenants. Ownership of Middle Hill for at least two hundred years (1672-1878) can possibly be attributed to the Savage and Phillipps family (see previous chapter). Over the years the farmhouse was developed even further to take advantage of the hugely profitable sheep and wool trade that proliferated at the beginning of the nineteenth century. Looking at the original irregular roof line for the main part of the house, it would certainly appear to have been extended upon over the years.

An early photograph, c.1965, of the ingle-nook fireplace, oak beamed ceiling and small window that probably dates to c.1700

Sir Thomas Phillipps inherited the estate from his father in 1818 and on his death in 1872, a dairyman named William Stock was the tenant of 'Knap Farm' with his family. Sir Thomas' daughter Henrietta then inherited the estate even though he had disowned her for eloping with James Halliwell in 1840 – an early protégé, but a suitor Sir Thomas did not approve of. Henrietta then placed the entire Middle Hill Estate up for sale in 1878, including 'The Knap Farm' comprising some 220 acres.

From Brewing to 'Baccy

The new purchaser of Middle Hill Estate was Edgar Flower of the well-known brewing family from Stratford-upon-Avon, who lived there until his death in 1903. Until then Elizabeth Savage, a widow, was living at 'Dornap' with her brother, Mickle Checketts, but on Flower's death his widow moved to 'Dornap' (being a Dower House; a widow's right to property after her husband's death) and Middle Hill was left unoccupied, although her nephew, Archibald, may have owned it as he was a significant landowner in Broadway. She was still living at 'Dornap' in 1924 and the Misses Hingley (three sisters) are believed to have bought the estate sometime after moving from the Elan valley in Wales, which was entirely flooded in 1904 to make way for the new dam system that ultimately supplied water to the entire Birmingham area.

The Hingley's were listed as leading landowners in the parish and one sister still resided at Middle Hill after the war ended in 1945.

From around 1950 the house was owned by the first Lord Dulverton of Batsford, Gilbert Wills (1880-1956); a member of the 'WD & HO Wills' family, the famous tobacco dynasty. His son Frederick Wills (1915-1992), the second Lord Dulverton and benefactor of Dor Knap to Toc H, was instrumental in the creation of the Overlord Embroidery.

This was a massive 227-foot long work commemorating the D-Day invasion on 6th June 1944 and inspired by the Bayeux Tapestry – coincidentally celebrating an invasion occurring in the opposite direction nearly 900 years earlier! The embroidery can be seen at the D-Day Museum in Portsmouth.

The last resident of Dor Knap before 1938 was Dr. Noel Davis who was listed as a member of the British Eugenics Society: right-wing, white supremacists and Nazi sympathisers. Dr. Davis was a Commissioner of Public Health in Shanghai and author of *Observations on Beri-beri in Shanghai*.

With reference to the ever-changing name, although the map on page 6 is just over 100 years old, it confusingly calls the house as 'Dornap'. But misnaming places and people was quite common in earlier times as most records were commonly documented according to phonetic sounds. Consequently, the house was named 'Dorn-Knapp, as seen in archives dated 1672.

The Conference Room (on left) was built in 1910. No other extensions were made until after 1979.

Dor Knap before Toc H occupation: 1938-1957

Throughout the war, the family of **Priscilla Joseph** were occupants of Dor Knap. Here is her story:

Our family rented Dor Nap[1] from the Middle Hill Estate from the autumn of 1938 to early in January 1945; most of the war in fact. My sister and her husband, who lived in East Africa, had taken it for a peppercorn rent as a home for my mother and their two sons: I was only there occasionally, when on leave from the children's hospital in London where I worked.

In spite of its deficiencies (and it had plenty) we all loved Dor Nap and as the war got more and more grim, found it a real refuge. At some time in the past the house had been 'modernised' and electricity had been installed – powered by the generator for Middle Hill – and central heating put in: but, by the time we got there, the generator could no longer carry the load and the boiler blew up the first time we lit it. The kitchen range was useless too, so we cooked on paraffin stoves, lit lamps and candles, and relied on fires in the sitting rooms for heat. We supplemented our coal ration by scouring the surrounding woods for fallen branches, but this was not approved of by the estate agent, who had no hesitation in saying so. However, no-one else collected it and it seemed to be a pity to waste good fuel, so the boys, revelling in this clandestine pursuit, got great pleasure in outwitting the chap and dragging home any they could find, cutting and stacking it in the woodshed.

The garden had once been glorious but when we got there it was overgrown and sadly in need of TLC. Both my mother and sister were keen gardeners but to begin with the kitchen garden was a problem. However with the assistance of an old gardener we eventually got it properly dug and throughout the war we never wanted for fruit and vegetables.

The only form of transport we had was our own feet but, to begin with, this made little difference as everything was delivered to the door: but with the war came petrol rationing and all such niceties stopped – even the milk had to be collected from the lodge by the main gates every day. Unless we went into Cheltenham by train and got a taxi back from the station, everything else (including our rations) had to be carried back up that long hill: but we were all good walkers and the boys were always happy to go on errands when at home. However, relying as we had to on paraffin for cooking and lighting, and hauling it up the hill became too much: eventually the Ministry of Fuel allowed us to have a tanker bring us our paraffin ration, twice a year.

In the summer of 1942 a great friend (Jacque Boutflower) took the cottage for herself and her family, to get them away from the Bristol air raids. Their husbands were, of course, away in the forces. At Christmas that year, my mother invited about half a dozen men from a local army camp to come and have a Christmas dinner with us on Boxing Day and, when she told Jacque and Betty about this, they joined in with enthusiasm, so both houses pooled their rations to make a huge plum-pudding and some mince pies.

[1] Priscilla still uses the spelling of "Dor Nap"

Left: The donkey stable was later converted to become the Chapel, c.1955

Betty's husband, who was stationed at Moreton-in-the-Marsh, managed to conjure up a huge turkey and cycled home on Christmas Eve with the thing strapped to his back. Vegetables and apples came, of course, from our own garden. Six Americans from a nearby camp accepted the invitation and I shall never forget the faces of those men when they came into the holly-hung house, saw the decorated table, and were served with a traditional dinner of turkey with all the trimmings, Christmas pudding and mince pies. One or two of the men brought their tea ration, so it was washed down with homemade ginger beer and gallons of tea. Then we played charades and good old party games.

Spies in the Attic

One night a stick of bombs straddled the local fields but, although noisy, they did no harm. However my mother was furious when, a day or so later, some voyeurs from Birmingham came driving by 'to see where the bombs had fallen so far out in the country'. "As if they hadn't enough bomb craters of their own to look at!" she blazed. Several people have asked me whether there really were spies in the house at one time, and the answer is "Yes"! I suppose they were only around for about ten days, but it seemed longer while it was happening. Pinpoint lights began to appear all over the Vale as it became dark and it was supposed these were guiding enemy bombers towards Coventry and Birmingham: eventually we managed to alert the police, the Home Office and an army unit stationed at Stanton.

For a few days it was my job to take reports over there, so that the army could get a picture of what was happening: those walks were long and a bit scary, but I survived and doubtless the exercise did me good. At night we listened to feet running through the yard and occasional sounds of scrambling as if someone was going over the roof. It all ended with a guest of ours being press-ganged by the army into guarding the family by sitting up all night with a twelve bore across his knees, while I sat beside him holding a torch to shine into the face of anyone coming upstairs. All night long we heard a cacophony of noises and scurrying feet round and over the house, but thank goodness neither he nor I had to use our weapons! For a further few nights a police guard spent the night there, then the whole thing went quiet: we learned later that two spies had been caught with a transmitter in a similar attic at Snowshill Manor.

D-Day was another day I shall never forget, when we spent the day watching in awe as planes and gliders gathered, manoeuvred and circled over the Vale, before finally setting off southward for somewhere. Our ears were glued to the news bulletins too, but the newscasters were silent and when it was quite dark, still listening to the planes overhead, we went off to bed.

1951-1957

Following the war it is possible the property was left vacant for a period of time — possibly because the Hingley sisters had all died — but in 1951 it was rented by Richard Mead who ran a coachwork business in Broadway. Apparently the house was barely habitable and needed a good deal of work — and even then some rooms were vacated because of rain seepage! Richard emigrated to South Africa in 1957 and two years later Dor Knap was home to Toc H.

How the house appeared around 1960, prior to the Terrace being fully developed.

Dor Knap – Toc H Life: 1959-1979

John Callf was a Toc H visionary. After a most distinguished service with the Indian Army, including the award of the Military Cross, John returned to the United Kingdom and took up an appointment with Toc H. Later he acted in a lay capacity with the Congregational Church. It seemed inevitable that John should return to the Toc H fold this time as the full-time Administrator, an office he filled with much success and great humility.

From the very beginning of his first appointment, John's great dream had always been that one day Toc H would be in possession of its own Conference Centre, though there were many perhaps who considered this no more than a mere pipedream on his part. The dream did in fact become a reality sooner than anyone could possibly imagine, including John, mainly due to a great friend of his, Richard Ayshford-Sandford. Richard resided at The Court, which stood on Snowshill Road just opposite the gateway that gave entrance to the long winding road that led up to Dor Knap. Richard was a member and Branch Treasurer of Toc H at Broadway.

Having lived at Dor Knap in his younger days, Richard knew the old house well. He also knew Lord Dulverton, a member of the Wills tobacco family, who owned so much of the land in those parts, especially at Batsford Park and Middle Hill. Unfortunately, over the years Dor Knap had gone into decline and had become unoccupied, beginning to fall into a near derelict state. Obviously heavy costs would be required to restore it.

In 1958 Lord Dulverton, concerned with the state of the house, offered it at a peppercorn rent to the Boy Scouts Association suggesting that they might use it as a "Midlands Gilwell Park". At first great interest was shown in this marvellous opportunity until it was noted that the long Cotswold tiled roof that covered the whole length of the property was in a very parlous state and would require complete replacement. Further consideration of this all-important factor suggested to the Scout Association that the costs involved were far greater than at first anticipated. After yet further consideration they withdrew completely from the project.

An early work party, c.1965. People of particular interest: John Callf (right), Tommy Trinder (left) and Jeff Christmas (sixth from left)

1959/1960 and the roof repairs get underway

That may well have proved to be the beginning and end of the story, except that at this point the friendship between Richard and Lord Dulverton began to really blossom so far as Toc H was concerned. Having got to know of the offer Lord Dulverton had made to the Boy Scout Association, and after consultation with John Callf, Richard enquired of Lord Dulverton whether or not he would be prepared to make the same offer, and at the same peppercorn rent, to Toc H – and much to the ecstatic joy of John and Richard, His Lordship speedily and readily agreed.

First Obstacles

The wheels began to turn and plans for the first Toc H Conference Centre were being laid. Once again however, the problem of replacing the main roof in a particular and specified style of tile proved a stumbling block to progress. As has often happened in the history of Toc H, the rescue came in the form of a friend of the Administrator; the Chairman of a large and well-known Northern Insurance Company personally offered to underwrite the cost of the new roofing involved. So the property was made weatherproof and parties, especially affiliated Schools parties, spent days and weekends on the restoration programme making the house habitable, largely under the guidance and spell of Alec Churcher, the then Schools Secretary of Toc H. It was only required of every visitor to make their contribution as they almost sweated blood on restoring house, grounds and the not-to-be avoided long, winding road. Through these efforts Dor Knap rejuvenated became "The House that Love Built".

The story of the development and the ultimate fulfilment of John Callf's dream may be read elsewhere in this publication, but all those over the following 20 years who fell in love with, and were won over by this old house, will remember with thanksgiving its peace, tranquillity, relaxation and depth of friendship. Some may even have scars to prove it! The bonds of friendship formed in work parties, in the Conference Room, the Snug, the Bothy (a small outbuilding for farm workers) and in the Chapel, live on and will never be readily forgotten.

As the first 20 years began to draw to an end the Dor Knap Committee approached Lord Dulverton to seek an extension of the lease beyond 21 years. But Lord Dulverton had already decided that the time had come for him to begin the process of sharing out his land and properties with his sons, and particularly that the Middle Hill Estate, including of course Dor Knap, should go to his younger son who would celebrate his 21st birthday during the final year of the existing lease held by Toc H.

Therefore His Lordship felt that his younger son should be the one to determine whether or not Toc H should have an extension, and if so at what rental.

1979: The end of an era

The reality of the situation quickly took hold, when, after many months of eager and hopeful anticipation, no word was forthcoming on any possibility of a lease extension, the Toc H Central Executive Committee (CEC) decided they could wait no longer. The Rev. John Hull, then Administrative Padre at Toc H HQ, was commissioned to search for an alternative to Dor Knap and eventually recommended to the Toc H CEC that possession be sought of Cuddesdon House, previously the home of the Bishop of Oxford, to become the new and much up-dated Toc H Conference Centre.

We pay our respects particularly at this time to friends such as John Callf, Lord Dulverton, Richard Ayshford-Sandford, Alec Churcher and all those who implanted on this lovely old house the imprint of love and depth of friendship that we all experienced there.

The booklet written by Alec Churcher describes the practical details for getting there with access from the North, South, East and West, but just as importantly it went on to outline the philosophy behind the centre and the activities that took place in this 'leadership training' centre which drew significantly on Alec's own publication *Stirring the Mixture* (nd) … 'learning from one another and from each other's experience'

At Dor Knap the physical demands made are not great, but over a period of time living together, a variety of responsibilities are constantly being put on one's shoulders and one is able to discover one's own unsuspected potential and to grow in confidence as a result.

Stories in the following chapters testify to these claims.

The well-known cast-iron sign, mounted below the Chapel bell housing

Dor Knap: the 'his and her' story of Toc H

As has already been intimated, all the activities associated with a period spent at Dor Knap had a profound affect on many people within Toc H. However, as a Movement that was born in the original Talbot House in Poperinge, Belgium, during the First World War, and re-born through houses known as 'Marks' across the UK, a belief in the value of residential experiences (a shared 'community') has always been central to the Toc H experience. Many 'camps', retreats, conferences, holiday weeks and weekends had played their part in the growth and development of the Movement, but this was always in someone else's property however much the ownership of the experience was rooted in Toc H.

One such example was Warden Manor in Kent where Toc H families shared some very special times. Several individuals who were to play a significant part in the development of Dor Knap first encountered Toc H there; one being George Lee. On its closure in 1979, the serving Wardens of Dor Knap, David and Clare Currant, became the first staff in the new centre at Cuddesdon. It must be emphasised that the Dor Knap experience and its Toc H life does need to be considered in the context of the Marks, Houses and Centres that made an impact on the life of the Movement.

At this point it must be noted that from the perspective of 2004 a joint Toc H Movement is assumed, but Dor Knap was originally established by 'the men' and very much considered a male preserve. It was not until 1967 when the Toc H Women's Association acquired their own training and conference centre; Alison House in Cromford near Matlock in Derbyshire.

Whilst searching for reminiscences for this publication there were several who claimed to be the first member of The Toc H Women's Association to share a Dor Knap experience. Apart from Warden's wives and Jean Taylor, the cook in the early days – we think we have got this right – that 'honour' actually belongs to Jennifer Mitchell, or Jennifer Lythgoe as she was then, as a member of the Bristol University Joint Group. A Clayton Volunteer in 1963, she attended the de-briefing event at Dor Knap that November and although the Volunteers were not actually part of Toc H they could 'use' the place as a one off booking – as Ken Prideaux-Brune testifies at the end of this publication; "the dam had been breached".

Within ten years or so the picture had changed dramatically, with week and weekend experiences automatically being assumed to be joint ventures. But this did radically affect the life of the house; not just how 'jobs' were decided but most of all how rooms were allocated…

Alison House, named after Alison McFie, founder of the Woman's Association.

Painting by David Newbould

The House Itself

Readers by now will have begun to appreciate many of the key exterior features of the house and grounds, and those who visited in 1979 could see how the original 'house' they may have visited in the previous 20 years had been adapted. Those who camped in the grounds in 1959 like John Jans, an Australian aide-de-camp to the Movement's Founder, the Rev. 'Tubby' Clayton (named as such after his rotund appearance), and the others who 'cleared a way' to the first entrances were able to see the potential of the house yet to be developed. A sketch map of the rooms that were 'usable' (we use the word advisedly!) in 1969, for example, would illustrate how the house was developing and what it would look like when handed back to the Dulverton family.

On entering the house from the main door on the lower terrace, the Conference Room was immediately to the left – a lovely long room that comfortably seated thirty. Impressive log fires roared in the winter and above the fireplace could be seen the striking painting of 'Tryfan' taken from an old Snowdonia railway poster.

Down one side was a grand couch, originally constructed by the furniture maker Gordon Russell in Broadway for King Feisal of Saudi Arabia, but when assassinated by his cousin it found its way up the hill to Dor Knap.

The gong in the hallway was to be found outside the appropriately named 'Snug', with its magnificent smell of wood smoke. Next to this was the dining room with its marvellous refectory table tops and their attendant benches that were (almost certainly) made at a London Police Court Mission home in Nutfield, Surrey where Toc H president Lance Prideaux-Brune was Chairperson. They had a very good carpentry instructor and the lads there made them under his supervision.

The legs of these tables were unusual as they had a mouse carved on them, and it is possible they were the work of the famous furniture maker Robert Thompson (1876-1955), who was known as 'Mousey Thompson' or 'The Mouse Man'. It is believed that when granted his first commission he was "as poor as a church mouse" and was so grateful he first produced this trademark as a sign of thanks.

On these tables were served sumptuous meals, often after a sung grace that reverberated under the low ceiling. The notoriously low ceiling also carried the often-ignored warning – "Duck or Grouse": in other words, "Duck your head or you will Grouse"! Many left with not only a full stomach but a severe headache as well!

Above: A modern example of a 'Mouse Man' carving

Left: The recognisable painting of the Welsh mountain, Tryfan, which could be seen above the fireplace

The hallway outside led to the small toilet and shower, and through the passage to the scullery where hilarity often echoed back down at washing-up times, or broke out up the steps to the top courtyard where a massive fig tree[1] produced very ripe fruit in some years.

Around this upper courtyard was the Wardens' House on the left, the wood store that later became a good-sized games room, and then the Chapel with its plain and simple furniture. Those that passed by could not fail to observe the sign made in wrought iron by Bob Strathman, a skilled craftsman from Croydon, and installed on the 9th of October 1971.

The bedrooms upstairs were sparse but serviceable, with one guest room having its own prized washbasin! There were more low-ceilinged rooms in the loft and also above the area leading out to the well-remembered and renowned Bothy (up some perilous steps), where ten bodies on bunk beds could be accommodated. Many tales have been recounted of late night excursions in the dark to find the nearest toilet after imbibing too well at the Crown and Trumpet in the village. The beds were constructed by 'Warmy' Warmington, who was employed by Toc H as their carpenter and furniture maker, and many recall they were built to be indestructible.

The hill at the back of the house, where badgers could be observed, was cut away to enable a damp course to be developed around this block. Where once there had been a tennis court, now a 'playing field' had been fashioned. The sketches offer some of us who saw Dor Knap in all its glories a clear reminder of how the house and grounds were developed.

On the main terrace the vista was tremendous and at its centre was located the amazing Toposcope – like a sundial but showing us where to look for the landmarks in the five counties spread before us. This was fashioned by loving hands at Wagstaffe and Appletons in Nottingham and their generosity enabled us, on a clear day, to pick out Snowdonia in the West, the Vale of Evesham in the foreground and the dark haze that was Birmingham in the North East.

Since 1959, many hundreds of Toc H members and young volunteers made their mark upon the place. Schoolboys from Bryanston in Dorset excavated the cartshed walls of the wood store, seniors of 70-plus re-tiled its roof, and South Staffordshire members under Norman Pursehouse converted it into a games room.

Lincolnshire members helped to reclaim the garden; Welshmen have rebuilt the terrace wall; and much of the plumbing was Scottish!

The upper courtyard looking towards the kitchen area. The Chapel can be seen on the extreme right with the bell housing protruding.

---

[1] Clare and David Currant recall; "Tommy Trinder added to the Friends of Dor Knap funds by occasionally flogging the ripe figs to the Lygon Arms in Broadway and we certainly enjoyed marvellous figs that last summer (1979)"

Left: The 'Teapot' can be seen in the right of this photo, in front of the terrace.

Essential work aside, it seems that a variety of people were responsible for the ever-evolving 'Teapot' (above). This was a large yew hedge at the end of the Conference Room that was trimmed religiously into the shape of a teapot.

Margery Knight recounts: "One special memory was of the bed quilts that had been knitted in squares of coloured wool and sewn together. They looked bright and right for the place – one thought often of the hours of love and dedication that went into producing them.

Not only the bricks and mortar, earth and water, flowers and trees, but myths and legends abound; "Were there really Nazi spies found in the old apple loft in World War Two; or were they escaped prisoners of war? And whose ghost was it really that flitted around after midnight?"

Below: During the colder winter months a regular supply of wood was required to 'keep the home fires burning'

Regular activities

Whenever one went to Dor Knap, the initial bone shaking climb up the rough, sometimes very rough, potholed road, often with whole sections washed away, gave a clue as to jobs the Warden might want doing. It became a tradition for mornings to be spent making a contribution to 'the estate' with regular gangs on the roads, gardens and walls – some becoming very proficient dry-stone wallers –once the courtyard parking area and the front had been sorted. Later on, work would start in the kitchen garden, but only once the 'sports area' had been made serviceable as a kick- about pitch – before the moles held sway!

It was always the intention that as far as was possible the general maintenance, and at times major repairs or even additions, should be done at minimal costs.

Always part of the Toc H philosophy was that of "the rent we pay for our room on earth" and therefore, in similar vein, all those enjoying the facilities of Dor Knap for whatever purpose, were expected to try and leave the house, in every respect, that much better than they found it. Many will call to mind the "chain gangs" and the continuing need for work parties that would help in particular, to maintain the mile-long winding road leading to Dor Knap from the Broadway-Snowshill main road.

From time to time there were special Work Parties, but in general the men were expected to do manual work whilst the women kept bed linen and the like in good order. There were many, of course, who made invaluable specific contributions and special mention should be made of Phil Jacques and fellow members of Bingham Branch; the parties from Mold Branch and elsewhere in Wales who, among other things, discovered the fresh water well by the corner of the Bothy.

Such parties were not only involved in general maintenance, but in major work involving the Games Room and the Chapel, the Scullery attached to the Dining Room, the Bothy, and eventually levelling the garden to provide an amphitheatre where the Cotswold Festivals later took place.

The hill behind the house with all the badger sets, provided the wood gatherers with their logs; for many a bough got caught in the strong south-westerlies that one experienced on reaching the corner of the drive, at the junction of the road between Broadway and Middle Hill.

No one seems to remember 'light duties' but many have recalled the ribald rivalry between the returning working parties as they gathered for the coffee and biscuits on the terrace. Regular visitors had particular spots around the house and grounds that held special memories, and tasks which people felt an identity with – even came back to visit. Many felt ownership of particular pieces of work in both house and garden.

Regular work parties were necessary to maintain and improve the grounds and the road leading to Dor Knap.

Regular patterns for the remaining programmes of events also fell into place: trips to Broadway, the Vale of Evesham, even Stratford-upon-Avon and Cheltenham for those who stayed longer than a weekend. Many haunts in the Cotswolds like Snowshill became popular too. The 'sessions' in the conference room used to start in late afternoon and after dinner there would be more talk of this and that. Sometimes a formal presentation would be given, sometimes in groups – the house could accommodate various permutations of group size.

On Sunday mornings there was usually a self-made service of hymns and readings in the chapel. If a Padre was amongst the number, the opportunity was there for an open table for communion, followed by more chat or chores and then usually a mammoth lunch before the homeward journeys began.

As Dor Knap proved itself an excellent base for project and 'volunteering' initiatives that were springing up all over the country in the middle 1960s, and aimed at introducing a younger element into the Movement, one activity that developed was "Night Exercises"…

Margery Knight writes: "One of the special things that many people remember was the "Night Exercises". Two adults would go out during the day and plant clues in the surrounding area – villages and hamlets included. Late at night two separate groups were taken to different spots some miles away and then had to make their way back to Dor Knap, finding and following the clues. They mustn't see or hear each other, but you would be surprised how much sound travels in the quiet countryside!

It took some hours for them to get back – across gardens, brambles, brooks, and so forth. We drove around in cars to make sure no noise came from the groups and if there was, points were lost. Finally, the teams would arrive back at Dor Knap footsore, weary and often bruised and bleeding but so pleased to be first. The second group always seemed to be worse off, but hot soup and bread were then served and I treated the injured before a very happy crowd finally dropped into bed.

There was one occasion when 'Tommy' Trinder[1] got lost in the woods during a pitch-black night. The teams had been split into 'Defenders' and 'Invaders' and whilst some 'Invaders' decided to approach the house from across the neighbouring fields, Tommy with his local knowledge decided

---

[1] 'Tommy' earned the nickname after the famous wartime comic and one-time chairman of Fulham FC.

Left: Entering the top Courtyard with the tiny Chapel ahead and adjoining Games Room, which replaced the wood shed.

the best approach was through the woods. All seemed to be going well, with everyone 'back home', until Dorothy noticed Tommy was still absent. Others began to share her concern when after half an hour he was still missing, and panic set in when after another hour he was still not answering his colleagues' calls. It was therefore with great relief when the arrival of a pale-faced and rather dishevelled Warden, who got completely disoriented in the blackness of the woods, brought that particular exercise to a conclusion. Phew! The Warden had at last found his way home…

The Terrace with its dry-stone walling, as built by Ivor Barker in 1961

Another time the parties camouflaged themselves, and one group near the hairpin bends on the hill down into Broadway heard a car go out of control. Not thinking about their appearance they found their way to the wreck – what must the young men in the car have thought when these wild people came to 'rescue' them!"

When studying the bookings at Dor Knap one notices that many of the weekends were shared with members from different areas, such as Bedfordshire and Hertfordshire (Beds. and Herts.) with the Southern Region. **Pat and Jack Turner** recall that when Colin Rudd, the Southern Region Padre (and mad motorcyclist), had to dash down to Southampton on a Saturday to officiate at a wedding. He returned to Dor Knap very late at night to find his slippers filled with paper and the bottom of his pyjama trousers all sewn up – just one of several bed-time stories we have been told. The men of Chard, recalls **Dennis Till**, had a penchant for going round, waking people up at some ungodly hour with a cup of tea, and asking if they "wanted to buy a battleship"!

Finally, John Burgess tells of a time in 1961 when Ivor Barker from Ryton in Northumberland was assistant Warden to George Atkinson and his wife Dorothy. A task Ivor undertook was to build a dry-stone wall around the Terrace and garden area. This looked easy, as he had seen many examples in the surrounding countryside and so painstakingly selected his stones and began work. This took some time due to his other duties in the House but finally it was completed and he stood back and admired his "Hadrians Wall". Very soon after it all fell down. Undaunted, he travelled to Stratford-upon-Avon, found a little bookshop and purchased a very old book on the art of dry-stone wall building. He cleared the site, started again, and this time was well pleased as he stood back to admire a class job well done.

It lasted the 20 years of Toc H life but was sadly dismantled sometime afterwards.

Special Events

The way Dor Knap developed led logically to some of the special events associated with the house. As well as the 'workcamps' (the early labour force contributed by Schools weeks, and matched by groups from Branches, Districts and Areas), there were Open Days for those who could not manage a whole 48-hour weekend, since more and more people in the Movement wanted to be part of the magic of the place.

There was the occasion when Alec Churcher – the party leader – spent most of a Saturday prior to the annual Dor Knap Open Day trimming a large bush near the Chapel, which was seriously straggly. By the end it was a good piece of topiary, looking very smart. That night two people crept out and spent ages carefully tying on most of the pieces he had so carefully cut off. The next morning, after breakfast, Alec was persuaded to inspect his handiwork of the day before! He was (briefly) speechless, then spluttered with indignation, as was his wont, and threatened to take out his teeth and gnash them!

Television Broadcast at Dor Knap

The enthusiasm generated by Dor Knap no doubt helped persuade the I.T.V. cameras to film at Dor Knap in 1961 for a forthcoming issue of the A.B.C. *Sunday Break* programme. This was a 'youth programme of the air' and filled a slot in the TV schedules on Sundays at 6.15pm. This particular episode, with the house being the main feature, was broadcast on 26th November 1961.

John Burgess recalls that on the Wednesday following this broadcast a young man named Keith Bowler walked into the local branch meeting. Keith had been so inspired by the programme this motivated him to find out more and he subsequently joined Toc H. John was particularly delighted as the number of members under 22 had just swelled from two to three!

Keith eventually obtained a position with Scotland Yard in London as a surveyor, and moved into the Mark XIII house. He finally emigrated to New Zealand.

Toc H and television were also involved together when 'Tubby' Clayton, the Toc H founder, was chosen as the guest for an episode of *This Is Your Life* (believed to be 1958) and presented by Eamonn Andrews.

There were International Weeks with members from across the globe, Warden's Weeks by special invitation and Seniors' Weeks. Tommy Trinder was a participant in one led by John Callf and later recruited as the longest serving Warden. Courses for Padres, 'Bordon Company' retreats and 'World Chain of Light' 24-hour Vigils all figured and later came exchanges with folk from Talbot House in Poperinge, Belgium, where Toc H all started. Family weeks were introduced with members and their families making the house a base for exploring the Cotswolds and beyond.

One Special Event was when members of the Bristol Caribbean Club visited Dor Knap in 1967/68

More adventurous weeks took place with members and their friends with disabilities – learning to negotiate the corridors, stairs and bunk beds. It hardly seems possible that all these activities developed quite quickly and led to other more sophisticated pursuits (see photo page 31).

A weekend led by Sue Sutton and Keith Rea (from Headquarters Finance Department) entitled "Accent on Poetry" led to a publication *The Poets of Dor Knap* (see *Point Three* magazine, October 1974). The original 'Painting Week' then became 'Painting and Music' Week, which ultimately led to the Cotswold Festivals, upon which a later chapter focuses.

The seeds of an idea

John Hull writes: "Painting and Music Weeks at Dor Knap began in 1968. It was Cyril Cattell's idea (General Secretary of Toc H at the time); Colonel John Davies, Chairman of the Central Executive and a superb watercolourist, was in charge of the painters and I looked after the music.

There were highlights too numerous to mention and the people who came to paint would find themselves making music, and vice versa. It is difficult to put into words what all this meant, but one thing I do know; many people experienced something new to them and I know of several people whose lives were changed because of it, and deep friendships were formed".

Sue Cumming writes: "When I joined the staff in 1973, John Hull had just begun to encourage people to explore the arts, and with the help of two artists had already held a couple of successful painting weeks at Dor Knap. He invited me to join him in Summer 1974 on a Painting and Music week, and they then really took off! The concept was simple – a group of people come to stay at Dor Knap and had the opportunity to have a go at painting and/or making music, whether or not they had ever done anything like it before. There was a painting demonstration between breakfast and coffee, and following this a choir practice. Afternoons were free to do anything you liked, and then after supper each evening there would be a talk on art or music.

The final evening was the occasion for each of the painters to show one of their masterpieces to the rest of the party, and for assorted musical items to be offered in a grand finale. The choir would sing; others would play solos or duets they had prepared during the week; one year we had a cello trio, and another year we got all the children involved in a performance of Haydn's Toy Symphony. Those who were there will never forget Nancy Griffiths doing her Joyce Grenfell recitations, John Hull's solo performances such as 'The Gas Man Cometh' by Flanders & Swann, or singing by Gill Cumming.

An early drawing: unknown artist but probably created during a Painting Week

The weeks were a great chance to discover a new streak of creativity, or indulge yourself with time to do things you were already practised at; singers discovered how good it was to spend time observing things whilst attempting to draw or paint them; artists enjoyed listening to music wafting through open windows; husbands and wives who came to accompany their artistic partners, found they got more out of 'having a go' themselves than they would have ever imagined.

I still remember Ken who came with his wife Edith, a painter. He listened to choir practice on the first day but declared himself tone-deaf. We encouraged him to have a go, and he joined in the concert at the end of the week, singing with the basses in a piece by Palestrina and various other arrangements for unaccompanied choir. The next year he told me he'd joined the local male-voice choir, and they were singing Messiah!

Again, it was the informality and ease of Dor Knap that soothed and stimulated tired or sad spirits, and breathed new life into people. There are far too many memories to record here, but many people were transformed by a week in the place, in the mixed company of people.

Correspondents remember Project Leaders Training Weekends, Winant and Clayton Volunteer Briefing events, a base for youth service group work exercises, a base for a touring cricket team, and regular Toc H staff meetings called 'Clumps' – and if you met with a staff team from another region it was known as a 'Ranagazoo' (such a lovely word). Anything was possible within the mixture of activities that developed the pattern that made Dor Knap so 'special'."

The Chapel

No one seems to know whether there was any special significance in the choice of room in which to establish the Chapel. Some of the early black and white photographs bring out the best of its powerful simplicity, convey its special serene atmosphere and remind us of its musty smell! The simple cross on the rough whitewashed wall, the bare wooden altar table modelled on a carpenter's bench under the bare beams, are all remembered by many.

Donkey Stable

The building itself was on the right of the entrance to the top courtyard and was originally a stable for donkeys. Perhaps with this thought in mind it became the natural choice for whoever chose it as a place of worship. Originally, the adjoining building was used as a wood store, but later got converted into a Games Room.

Below: The Chapel with James 'Noddy' Thornbury ringing the bell to call everyone to morning prayer during a Warden's Week, c.1965

Above: The chapel conveyed serenity with its simplicity. Rather poignantly the building used to be a donkey stable

The Master Carpenter

O Christ, the Master Carpenter, who at the last through wood and nails, purchased man's whole salvation, wield well Thy tools in the workshop of Thy world, so that we, who come rough-hewn to Thy bench, may here be fashioned to a truer beauty by Thine hand. We ask it for Thy name's sake.

Below: The Rev. Bob Knight with wife Margery at the Toc H 60th Jubilee celebrations. On the left is the Dean of Poperinge.

Without doubt, Bob was the most influential padre at Dor Knap

With a full party of 28 everyone could get in 'at a push'. The singing had to be unaccompanied and any pattern of worship needed to cater for a wide range of tastes. From 1963 to 1975 Bob Knight as HQ Padre was particularly influential in encouraging the use of the chapel and his *Yours is the Glory* (Published by Toc H, in 1971), rapidly becoming standard reference for 'Prayer in Toc H', and when this went out of print he produced "Joyful Journey" (Toc H, 1982). Anyone opening this text will recognise many of the patterns of readings, prayers and songs that were used in the Chapel over these 20 years, summed up best perhaps by 'The Master Carpenter' on page 116.

Tales of Dor Knap

Like any movement, Toc H developed its own language and acronyms – 'Ranagazoo' was probably one of the most extreme. In any booklet such as this many will have to be explained. The 'Bordon Company' was the prayer fellowship developed by members who took the name of the Hampshire town where the idea was first mooted. The World Chain of Light, a Vigil to keep a Toc H Lamp alight for a full 24 hours somewhere in the World whilst members came together over the 11th and 12th December each year – Tubby Clayton's birthday and the anniversary of the opening of the original Talbot House.

The significance of some stories may be difficult to convey 25 years on, and similarly it is hard to convey something of the early Toc H craftsmen. One with a link to Warden Manor was Harry Cromack from Leatherhead who left his mark around the house, not least as the 'master carpenter' who oversaw the construction of the basic furniture and altar in the Chapel.

Cyril Cattell recalls a party to Dor Knap in the very early days that included Harry. "We found a large piece of oak in the grounds and made it into the chapel cross; it seems that a 17 year old lad actually created it, but with Harry sitting beside him throughout gently telling him how! The lad was bursting with pride at what he had achieved!"

John Callf also had an able and enthusiastic lieutenant in the shape of Alec Churcher, its Training Officer, who wrote the original pamphlet. There was John Jones the marvellous Padre raconteur from North Wales who 'sold' the house to countless people who made their mark on the house from that part of the world over the years, as did the 'mighty midget' Johnnie MacMillan from Bristol.

Integration

Once the Toc H Men & Women Associations became integrated, women began to make their own individual contribution to the house, particularly Mary Edwards who became chairperson of the Dor Knap committee, and Frank and Dorothy Kirk, the key members of the 'Friends of Dor Knap'.

Our correspondents have bombarded us with stories of characters far too numerous to mention, who made their mark on the life of the house. One story probably encapsulates many of the facets of the Dor Knap experience as related by Ray Fabes (overleaf).

Frank Kirk (left) who founded 'The Friends of Dor Knap', seen here with Tommy Trinder

Early Days

Ray Fabes writes: "The first recollection of hearing the words 'Dor Knap' was when, as a new councillor, I heard the negotiations had been completed at the Central Council in 1959. So exciting! The Movement was to have its own centre – no more residentials in other organisation's establishments. A working party was organised back in my own Branch where I was 'Jobmaster' at the time, and a few of us hot-footed it to Broadway only to discover it was the week that Wilf the first Warden had died so local members put us up.

The next Easter, 1960, when I had joined the full-time staff, I co-led a Schools Week with Ken Prideaux-Brune (later to become Director). I remember collecting young men from one of our Affiliated Schools, Calday Grange in the Wirral, and driving them down with none of us knowing what to expect from a week in what we thought was a tumble-down farmhouse. I don't remember what we did except I've still got a photo of the group – but no idea of any names! I just recall that on the last night I was press-ganged into doing a Max Bygraves' impression; "They've turned our local Palais into a bowling alley, and fings ain't what they used to be …"

For many of us every time we came to Dor Knap that was very true.

Sue Cumming writes: "Schools week, Easter 1965 – an extraordinary collection of people, and an extraordinary experience which had a profound impact on me. The participants came from a wide range of backgrounds: Richard from public school, Colin from a 'Tech' (having left Secondary Modern at 15), Erica from a nice Girls' Grammar School, Kath and me from a mixed Grammar School in the Midlands, and others whose names I now can't recall.

Ray Fabes was heavily involved in several Youth Projects at Dor Knap. Pictured here in 1968 with disabled members.

We arrived at this rather ramshackle building at the end of the long, bumpy, winding drive up the hill ('Are you sure this is the right way?' asked the driver, rather nervous about his car). The girls were sleeping in bunks in the Bothy; in those days access was outside at the back: I can't remember where the loo was, but it wasn't *en-suite*! Heating was provided by log fires downstairs – we had to chop the wood up first – but the inglenook fireplace in The Snug smoked terribly and it was still cold, so we sat on each other's knees to keep warm (what a great excuse!) as we ate Dorothy Trinder's chocolate biscuit cake and drank tea out of large pot mugs. The chimneys were not the only things that smoked.

There were talks, walks and discussions, and a mad night exercise that would be banned these days on Health and Safety or Insurance grounds! Working together in the garden, reclaiming it from brambles and nettles – excavating a flight of stone steps, and shrubs, which in years to come, though unbeknownst to me at the time, would be such familiar parts of the landscape on Painting and Music weeks and Cotswold Festivals, and many other occasions which took me to Dor Knap. We peeled potatoes in a machine, supervised by Tommy Trinder, and shared the washing-up after the meals. One afternoon we tickled Colin to death – just as Bob the Padre came into the room who then obliged by sticking a daffodil in Colin's navel and conducted a mock funeral, which came to a hysterical end when the 'corpse' laughed.

I still vividly recall the simple service of Holy Communion on Easter Sunday in the chapel (formerly a donkey stable), with whitewashed walls and a carpenter's bench as the altar – with fermented wine in the shared chalice (a bit of a shock for a young Methodist!).

I was bowled over by the glorious mixture of fun and serious concern for the world and other people; by being taken seriously as a person, and liberated to be me; by being cared for when I went down with a 24-hour flu bug ('Do you want to go home early, Sue?' – not on your life!!!); by meeting such a wide mixture of people, some Christian, some Communist, some nothing in particular – but finding we all cared about similar things; by being allowed to ask what Christianity was really all about – and having it confirmed that it wasn't just about going to church or being a good girl. What a relief!

I found myself thinking that I had found something – people, a spirit, a set of ideas – I had hardly dared to hope existed. It was a glimpse of the love of God in ordinary human beings. It felt like the pearl of great price. Much later I found some words written by Bishop Iranaeus in the 3rd century – *'The glory of God is a human being fully alive.'* How good it was to begin to come to life that Easter."

Second encounters

Sue continues: "Autumn 1973 – the diary said 'Ranagazoo – Dor Knap'. I looked forward to it, though I knew it would be different. What was a Ranagazoo? No idea, apart from the fact it was a 24 hour-long staff meeting for Toc H staff in the Midlands and South West. I must have been the only female, and certainly I was the youngest, and newest member of staff. I hadn't the faintest idea what they were talking about half the time (staff or membership matters, or policy issues) – it got quite intense at times, until at one point John Hull exploded with laughter and said, "What a load of old socks!

A party maintaining the road and fences leading to Dor Knap – a regular and necessary task.

A well-earned break during a days hard slog!

'Blow the Wind Southerly'

David Wakefield writes: "It must have been around 1960 or 1961 when I was invited to go along on an experimental week at Dor Knap. The idea was that four 'men' of around the same age who knew what Toc H was (we couldn't be members as we weren't 18) would go to Dor Knap with 'men' of about the same age who were apprentices, four from Rowntrees, and four from Reckitt and Coleman's. The week was organised by the Rev. Ron Smith who at that time was on the Toc H staff, working in the Yorkshire region.

I agreed to go on this week with rather mixed feelings. My parents were both members of Toc H and had been since the 1920s. Our house revolved around Toc H, Hospital libraries, choirs being organised in hospital wards housing the terminally ill, for example.

Part of being a teenager was to be 'anti-parent' and all they stood for, so I viewed Toc H with a wary eye. I had met Ron Smith before and he sold me on the idea of going, as I found him a very approachable person with a great sense of humour; far different to any clergyman I had ever met and far different from my perception of the average Toc H member!

We went by car and met the others when we arrived at Dor Knap – a good crowd who mixed well right from the start. I can't remember the names of the Wardens at that time, only that they joined in everything that we did and were great fun. The meals were superb! One thing I do remember about the Warden's wife was that she was related to Kathleen Ferrier [Dorothy Atkinson's sister, Eds.] and was immediately impressed, as her singing of 'Blow the Wind Southerly' was one of my favourite songs.

The air was usually thick with smoke (pipes were almost *de rigueur*) but they had got the heating sorted a bit better by then, and I wasn't out in the Bothy this time. It was great to be back.

There were further Ranagazoos before we were reorganised into Staff Clumps. On another occasion one Spring, there was a faint dusting of snow on the ground, which was no worse until we got to Chipping Campden. By this time the snow was a bit heavier, and there was a strong wind blowing the snow across fields, and through gateways. We decided to go over the top of the hill, past Broadway Tower, rather than down into Broadway and then struggle up the hill from the bottom. Just beyond the crossroads on the main road we saw the snow blowing through a gateway ahead – but didn't see the snowdrift which lay beyond it. The nose of the car embedded itself, and try as we might we could not get the car free – the snow was building up around it faster than we could kick it away. It took a four-wheel drive vehicle, and John Mitchell arriving with a spade and two pieces of carpet to go under the wheels, before we got the car free. A salutary experience. For the rest of my time on Toc H staff I had a spade and a piece of carpet in the boot of my car each winter, just in case!"

The weekdays followed the same pattern. After breakfast we all collected shovels, pick-axes and a wheelbarrow, walked down the track and then, half way between the house and the road, we did road repairing. It was hard work but a good laugh too. How we looked forward to the sight of the Warden at mid-morning, who appeared with flasks of tea, home made ginger beer and biscuits.

The meal at night was always something everyone looked forward to after the hard day and the country air. I came from Sheffield, two of the Toc H-ers came from Leeds, one came from Tadcaster, the Rowntree lads all came from York, and the Reckitts' lads came from Hull.

The evenings varied: on some evenings we discussed a topic with Ron Smith, with the Warden and his wife joining us; on other nights we walked down to Broadway and went to the nearest pub, The Crown and Trumpet.

One evening a really special event occurred when, at about 8.30pm, Tubby Clayton turned up[1]; I remember that he had been to some event in the Midlands, knew about this special week and on his way back to London decided to call in at Dor Knap. Talking went on until about 2am. He wanted to know all about us, where we came from, our jobs, background and so on. I was fascinated to meet the person who I had heard my parents talk about so much and on returning home they were quite envious of my experience.

All too soon the week came to an end. I found muscles I didn't know I had due to the road repairing work, had met and shared a week with some fascinating people of my own age, and in Ron Smith had met someone who was going to shape the rest of my life, even if neither Ron nor myself knew it then!

On returning to Sheffield I became a full member of Hallam Branch of Toc H, taking my turn in carrying out the jobs that the Branch did. A few years later my work in Local Government took me to Bromsgrove where I became a member of Alvechurch Branch. Whilst there I started a scheme at a local school for blind children where they could play cricket and football against sighted volunteers. Volunteers also took a number of blind and partially sighted children to football matches in Birmingham and commentated for them. I am relating this, not to blow my own trumpet, but to demonstrate what that week at Dor Knap led to. My voluntary work in Toc H led me to train as a social worker, which I did for 17 years specialising in child abuse work, and this in turn led me to answering the call to go into the Church of England Ministry where I have specialised until recently in Prison Chaplaincy.

Little did I know when I went on that excellent week what it would lead to."

Tubby Clayton was a frequent visitor. Pictured here in the Conference Room, talking with Ted Tunnadine (right) after a conference.

---

[1] It was quite common for Tubby to turn up unannounced at any time, night or day. This meant the Warden had to rush round finding a bed for him – even when they were fully booked!

Gwyn Harvey writes: "My first brief encounter with Toc H was as a young teenager visiting London with my parents. During our sightseeing tour we popped into All Hallows by the Tower. About the only thing I remembered was the Toc H lamp on its stand. Somehow it fascinated me. It was more than a decade later that I rediscovered Toc H, when I married into what could only be described as a Toc H family, the Harveys of Netherton in Worcestershire. Bob Harvey, as a lad, used to go to the Toc H meetings with his father and there they came to know John Callf who, as a young man, served as a staff member for the West Midlands Region.

Come the Jubilee Year of Toc H in 1965, it came to Bob's notice that John Callf, now Administrator of Toc H, would be leading a Pilgrimage to the Holy Land. We simply *had* to go. The following year we 'pilgrims' were invited to join the Bordon Company – a group of Praying Members – for their annual retreat to be held at Dor Knap and which John would be leading. And thus, on 20 May 1966, we first discovered Dor Knap.

As we approached Broadway we continued to the right along the Snowshill road until we came to the Church and then the gateway inviting you through to Dor Knap. But *where* had we come to? As we continued up the long winding drive with its deep potholes and ruts, and our poor car scraping over the bumps, we wondered what we were doing there! But then that last bend and the glorious view over the Vale of Evesham. Nothing else would surely matter now! A knock on the door and a good old Cockney welcome awaited us from Tommy, the Warden, and his wife Dorothy. We were shown to our little room, up those narrow stairs and to the back of the building, with its tiny window facing the fields, in the old original part of the house. What if there was a fire? Seemingly no escape from here – but yes; all one needed to do was open the little window, cast out the rope provided for the purpose and slide down it – what more could you want! All our real needs were catered for us here at Dor Knap.

At breakfast the following morning, sitting at those long tables in the Dining Room, we ate our cornflakes and Tommy's special 'burnt bread' as he called it (toast of course) and felt we had arrived.

We were hooked and knew we would have to come again. During that weekend we also did some work in the garden between sessions and it was all over too quickly.

Our next visit was the following Easter for a 'Painting and Bird Watching' long weekend. Colonel John Davies, a very talented watercolourist, led the artists and we painted views around the house before venturing further down the drive to the woods. Although it was at the end of April, it was bitterly cold and flasks of coffee were brought down for us to warm up a bit. Yes, it was cold, but it had to be the start of something.

The dining room with its long tables led to a more informal communal approach

A sketch of Dor Knap by Col. J. A. Davies, a former Toc H Central Executive Chairman

And indeed the following year, towards the end of August, a whole week was booked for painters again but this time a 'Music and Painting Week'. John Davies led the painters again and John Hull was in charge of the Music – the start, for us, of a long friendship with him. The seeds were planted and these weeks continued right to the end of the Dor Knap years. When by 1972 John Davies felt no longer able to lead the whole week, a young man, Ian Dawson, took over for a few years with John just giving a few demonstrations.

Then, in 1975, Bob and I were invited to 'look after' the painters, going around making 'encouraging noises' to the others. In 1976, one week had swelled to two when the now renowned painter, Moira Huntly, who still lives in the nearby village of Willersey, came up several times to give demonstrations. A crescendo was reached by 1977 when we met for two weeks at the end of July and for another week at the end of October. A few intrepid painters went for a week during February 1978, and it was indeed cold then, followed by another that October. Moira was still coming to us to give her wonderful demonstrations.

But we were nearing the end. One last week was held during October 1979. We were all invited down to Richard Ayshford-Sandford's home during that week for a drink at teatime, and that was it. We finally said 'goodbye' to Dor Knap.

Interspersed between the Painting and Music weeks, Bob and I also went on Family Working Party Weeks there in 1968, 1969 and again in 1970 and 1975 from his newly-formed Branch of Llanarmon-yn-Iâl in the Welsh hills.

So what are my special memories? They all come flooding back. I remember the night when all good people should have been in bed long since, to hear a loud banging noise echoing through the house. Someone had summoned long-suffering Tommy because they had noticed a dangerous nail in the floor of the landing. So Tommy came with a hammer there and then – and what better time is there to do anything than *right now*! I remember those idyllic coffee breaks on the terrace overlooking that fabulous view. Evening sessions in that beautiful Conference Room with a roaring log fire. Work Parties building walls and weeding the flowerbeds. Washing up in that huge earthenware brown sink in that dark little scullery (how on earth did Tommy and Dorothy manage all they did in those primitive conditions?)

There was that glorious sunny day sitting at my easel in the garden down below the house when it was 'coffee up' time on the terrace. By the time I returned a cow had broken through the hedge – such inquisitive creatures – and was apparently contentedly munching at my picture!

There were the Friday nights during the Painting and Music weeks when we had a concert and a display of some of the paintings we had produced so as to share our achievements with the others. Oh, those evenings and how we enjoyed them! Some wonderful work was produced by people who had never indulged in either music or painting before.

All these incidents were surely part of the whole magic of Dor Knap, where people went, often as strangers, and left at the end of a week knowing more about their fellow men (and women) and about the things that really matter in life. I recall John Hull, a talented artist in his own right, once saying that while trying to paint something as 'humble' as a Brussels sprout, how one can see its beauty for the first time, and that is how one begins to understand the beauty of character even in an unlikely person. That is what Toc H is all about.

This is just a glimpse of the very special spirit engendered in that wonderful place."

Flagging Conflicts

Margery Knight writes: "Dor Knap for me was not just a retreat but also a place for hard work.

We went with groups of young people for 'retreat' times where they had structured discussions and also deep, totally unexpected 'talk' times, many until the early hours of the morning. In fact I often wondered if they ever slept.

The times I most remember are Easters and Whitsuns, when for many years we met whichever youth group had agreed to garden and clean up after the winter. Some years it was Toc H youngsters and on others it was Scout groups. One Scout group from the Southern area stands out in my mind for their hard work and fun. They arrived on the Friday then proceeded to hoist the Union flag and Scout flag up the flagpole. It was a hot weekend and they worked so hard, but with constant jokes and fun and also a quiet time in the chapel.

On the Sunday afternoon a coach-load of Welsh singers arrived [believed to be the Llwynegrin Singers and the date 24th May 1970, Eds.] – and then the real fun started, though at times it felt like war! Down came the Union and Scout flags, up went the Welsh flag, and tempers flared.

There was also trouble at meals as the Welsh men decided they had first sitting and sang their grace. Before they could get out, in rushed the youngsters who proceeded to sing their Scout songs.

It was a really funny weekend though I don't think the Welsh choir appreciated it. When their coach was about to leave, out rushed the boys with the roller and held up departure by a final roll of the drive!

The Amphitheatre was probably the most ambitious project, but it proved to be an amazing success when hosting the Cotswold Festivals. Work began in 1965 and it was ideally situated just below the Terrace.

It was a number of projects that created the amphitheatre and seats cut into the grass slope down from the drive and finally a stone and concrete platform. It was a great experience working on it but even more wonderful to sit on those seats on a summer evening, listening to beautiful music and watching the colours of evening across the valleys".

That Welsh Lot!

Bob Harvey writes: "Those who have been to Dor Knap in the 'old days' will remember that Tommy put a book in the entrance hall open for the next party and the length of their stay. Everyone had to sign it.

So surprise, surprise – on our page was the heading:

'Llanarmon-yn-Iâl Branch' That Bloody Lot!

So how did we come to deserve that reputation?! Our Branch, as you might imagine, came from the hills of Wild Welsh Wales – a land of grey stone and slate – so how natural that we should bring the feeling of Welshness to Dor Knap.

This we did by building stone walls; wherever Tommy wanted a wall, we built him one. The ladies of the party meanwhile were weeding the flowerbeds or painting outside doors all round the house. Now, on our previous week we had been joined by Conway Branch and a notable member of Conway[1] Branch was one Jonathan Parry, a slightly built Welsh speaker with twinkling eyes. Jonathan's main claim to fame was that he was a Master Mason and was in complete charge of all the renovations, repairs and maintenance of Conway Castle. So he knew a thing or two about stone walling and you may rest assured that all walls around Dor Knap were soundly built!

Maybe when Tommy was writing the heading on our page in the entrance hall book, he had already got a somewhat jaundiced view of the impending Welsh invasion, because he knew (from the previous year) that he'd be chasing up and down to Broadway all week, getting more – and yet more – sand and cement for those wallahs up at Dor Knap!

I happened to be passing by one morning where Jonathan was keeping a fatherly eye on a younger member of Llanarmon when I heard him say, in his broad Welsh accent, 'Now, look here lad, if you're going to leave a hole in your wall big enough for a rat to get in, make it big enough for a ruddy cat to get in after it, isn't it?'

It was hard going, especially as time was limited for what we wanted to do. Large stones are very heavy, and trips to the First Aid Box for treatment of squashed fingers were frequent. The mortar-mixers were kept hard at it too, and carrying the mortar to the wallahs was backbreaking; buckets of wet mortar are very heavy. But it was a great joy with laughter and leg pulling never far away.

---

[1] 'Conwy' was the original spelling, but was Anglicised when the railway ran through—the name has now reverted back.

Left: On entering Dor Knap, all visitors and members of a party were required to sign the Visitors Book

I guess that by lunchtime we'd earned a bit of a sit down on the terrace, savouring that superb view over the Vale of Evesham with a can or two of our favourite tipple – on a fine day we could almost see home to North Wales from up there!

Dor Knap was a place of many facets and this contributed largely to its charm and fascination. You had the peace and serenity of the lovely little Chapel and the rather more noisy Games Room, which in the Painting Week found itself acting as a studio for and budding Michelangelo. Here Llanarmon made full use of the Snooker Table in spite of a crudely stitched up tear in the green baize.

In the evenings after dark we could see some aspects of the wildlife, when Tommy emptied the remains of the day's meals at a place at the back of the house, and we could watch badgers – lots of them and all ages – come down to feast. You could shine powerful torches on them and they didn't mind. Also, more unusual, in a certain little spot at the side of the house, you could see glow-worms all lit up – a very unusual sight.

It was, above all, a place where you could let your hair down and relax, and in the evenings Llanarmon and Conway did just that. It's strange how we used to gather round the long tables in the Dining Room rather than the Conference Room. Maybe it was because the rather grand Conference Room with its chairs all round the outside walls was not as cosy as the Dining Room – where we were all closer together – and in any case, it was much nearer to Tommy's Bar; most important!

We did have a birthday at Dor Knap, that of Llanarmon member, Amos. So we made him a cake complete with icing and a candle and set it in front of him with a large knife. Amos commenced to cut the cake – or at least he tried to. He tried really hard before realising he'd been 'had' and the cake was solid concrete! 'It's stone, you beggars', cried Amos… but we had arranged a proper one for him as well!

What happened in the evening was anybody's guess. It could be boisterous – especially when somebody found he'd had some holly leaves pushed down his bed. And there was plenty of story telling and reminiscing, particularly as the evening wore on and the contents of Tommy's Bar loosened people's tongues!

But it wasn't all talking and noise. It couldn't have been a Welsh Week without some singing and Tommy, on his way through the Hall, must have paused to listen as the strains of that loveliest of Welsh Hymns – Calon Lan – flowed gently through the old building.

What the 'Welsh Lot' were good at: building walls! Note the 'Teapot' in the background. Photo taken in April 1960

Strange Coincidences

Bertha Smith writes: "My weekend there, not long before it closed, led to an extraordinary coincidence. We were asked to get into groups and tell something of our lives and I happened to mention where I went to elementary school, 60 years before. Afterwards a couple came up to me and the husband said he was sure he was in my class at the school. On giving his name I recognised him immediately and then asked if he knew what had become of my particular friend of those days – only to be told that she was his sister-in-law!

We found we were living within five miles of each other and a re-union was arranged. We all happened to be members of Holiday Fellowship, which led to spending some holidays with them. When I moved to Lymington they all spent holidays with me until my friend died a few years ago. If it hadn't been for Toc H, and my visit to Dor Knap, none of this would have happened."

Wildlife proliferated around the house and badgers took full advantage of Tommy's generosity!

'sKnapshots'

Some 'sKnapshots' from **John Mitchell**: "… watching badgers by the back gate. Tommy Trinder fed them each night, and one could sometimes see six or seven eating together. Though disturbed by noise, they responded to flash bulbs with a baleful stare.

… afternoon tea on the terrace in the sunshine, eating our way through mounds of Dorothy's wonderful 'hedgehog cake', the recipe for which originally came from Australia.

… standing on the terrace one summer night watching a rolling thunderstorm work its way up the Vale, past Evesham. One flash of lightning was followed by a bright blue flash from the ground and every light in the Vale went out! So this was how the blackout must have looked.

… The disbelief of many of our party of young men when we realised that the person who was plaguing us each night with apple-pie beds was none other than the respected, elderly, erudite group leader – Alec Churcher. He was suitably punished!

… Gales of laughter from the cramped, totally unsuitable, washing-up area.

… The nightmare of needing to visit the loo in the night when sleeping in the Bothy – necessitating an outside trip (sometimes through rain or snow) to the detached toilet.

… Putting the world right in the early hours of the morning, close round a fire blazing in the inglenook in the 'Snug'.

… The deep night silence, with the occasional hoot of an owl or a fox barking… and then the noisy dawn chorus of the rooks in the stand of trees higher up the hill."

By men, for men...

Reflections on Dor Knap from **Ken Prideaux-Brune**: "Thinking of my first experiences of Dor Knap I am reminded how different the world was of more than 40 years ago. When Dor Knap was acquired Toc H and the Toc H Women's Association were separate organisations. They worked together in many ways but there was also a quiet undercurrent of competition between them. As Joyce Green comments, 'Wimmin were not initially welcome' but due to Dor Knap's success the Women's Association acquired their own centre in 1967 at Alison House, in Cromford, Derbyshire – anything you can do, we can do better. They set up the Alison House Trust to own it, so as to ensure that if at some future date the two organisations united, Alison House would not fall under the control of the men (!)

And Dor Knap was set up by men, for men. Only men would be allowed to stay there, but I'm afraid I broke that cosy arrangement. The first official group of Clayton Volunteers spent the summer of 1960 working with churches and community organisations in the rough, tough Lower East Side of New York. I asked John Callf, the Administrator of Toc H and the man who conceived and developed Dor Knap, if I might take the Clayton Volunteers to Dor Knap to reflect on their New York summer. The request caused consternation. On the one hand this was precisely the kind of event for which Dor Knap was intended; but on the other hand this was a mixed group, and this was definitely not allowed. Eventually, a sort of compromise was reached. Since the Clayton Volunteers were not legally part of Toc H, I would be allowed to use Dor Knap for their weekend, so long as it was clearly understood this was not to be regarded as a precedent!

But in fact, of course, the dam had been breached. Within a short time the programme of short-term residential projects, all of which attracted both women and men, began; and many of them took place at Dor Knap. And Dor Knap was also used for the training of future project leaders, as well as for debriefing sessions for the returned Clayton Volunteers each autumn. Somehow, we always reached Dor Knap after dark on the Friday evening, but then the next morning, looked out on that incredible view, across the Vale of Evesham to the Malvern Hills and even, on a very clear day, the hills of Wales; and they began to breathe in the very special atmosphere that was Dor Knap. I vividly recall one extraordinary morning. Dor Knap was above the clouds in bright sunshine. The whole Vale of Evesham was a great white sea of cloud, with just the occasional peak poking through. But that view was always an inspiration, even on cold grey winter days.

Reflecting on so many happy times at Dor Knap is a nostalgic exercise – but let us not get carried away – the place was very much of its own time. When Toc H finally received notice to quit, many people were already unhappy about the cramped and crowded conditions and the inadequate toilets. This kind of close quarters communal living was no longer as acceptable as it had been 20 years earlier. Today it is unimaginable – without extending the building, which might have been expensive and might well have destroyed its special atmosphere, it would have been hard to attract either guests or staff. So let us celebrate its 20 remarkable years without pretending that its closure was a disaster. Since then there have been happy memories of its successor, Cuddesdon House."

Painting and Music Week 1979 (Dor Knap – Hail and Farewell)

The last reminiscence is an extract reproduced from an article written by Cec Griffiths in *Point 3* magazine and published during Toc H's last year of tenure at Dor Knap.

'Let's go to Dor Knap on a Painting and Music week for our holiday this year' I suggested to Joan.

'What's Dor Knap – and what do we know about music or painting?' she responded (she's always a bit suspicious of anything new when it comes to holidays.)

I explained to her that Dor Knap was the old farmhouse in the Cotswolds which had been let to Toc H by Lord Dulverton nearly 21 years ago when it was little better than derelict, that the members had rallied together to make it habitable and that ever since then many members of Toc H had made a yearly pilgrimage. Many had been the tale told of the beauty of the countryside and of the breathtaking view from the house; but more importantly, the fellowship, friendship, comradeship of everyone who had ever visited Dor Knap was legend. Joan was beginning to warm to the idea, so I kept talking and it wasn't long before I had convinced her that even novices such as we could join in. In any case, it said in the projects booklet that we would be welcome if we could only stand and stare – we could do that, anyway! So she fell for it, and I had the application form off before she could recant; we waited about three or four weeks and then heard we were in. By this time Joan was becoming enthusiastic, and some of this enthusiasm rubbed off on to Rob, (He's 18 and waiting to go to university). So I wrote again to see if there was room for him, and luckily there was.

Came the day and off we set to Broadway feeling a little apprehensive – especially Rob. The rough track up to the house was certainly not exaggerated — Rob was driving and I felt fearful for the car's back axle, since a mountain torrent was pouring down the middle of the track, which appeared to have a gradient of about one in seven. We wended our way slowly up the hill, and gradually I relaxed sufficiently to notice and appreciate the view. Breathtaking was right. Joan was completely sold. My choice of holiday was vindicated!

Our arrival at Dor Knap was met by a wave from a complete stranger who was walking across the lawn. There was an absence of doormen or porters to take our luggage, but by the time we had made the acquaintance of two children who told us where the dining room was situated and discovered that tea was being served we felt at home. 'I'm Griff and this is Joan' I told the harassed looking man behind the teapot in the kitchen. 'Hallo, Joan and Griff – I'm David' was the response. We had arrived and we were among friends.

There was a party of 30 people (including two leaders, John Hull and Sue Cumming), seven children and seven 'teenagers and the rest of uncertain age like ourselves. The days had a fair mix of music and painting, including demonstrations of painting by a local artist, Moira Huntley, who made it all seem so easy that even I decided to have a go (I produced Dor Knap on a foggy night!). Dor Knap

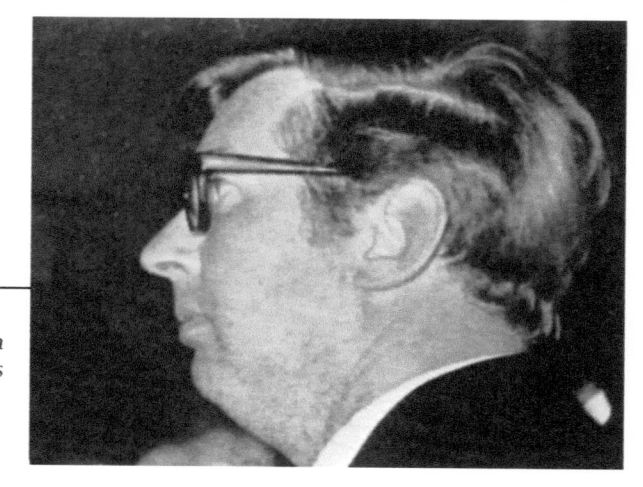

John Hull was a popular leader during Painting & Music Weeks and instigated a Singing Group for the Cotswold Festivals

resounded at almost every moment of the day to piano, violin, recorders, glockenspiel, 'cello and the human voice. In every vantage point and nook and cranny it was possible to observe budding artists with their easels set up, busy on their latest masterpiece – and there were many of the party who really had talent. The 'teenagers and the children got on with each other like a house on fire – there was never a dull moment. If you can imagine a lovely sunny day with the bees buzzing, a farmer making hay in a field nearby, the lounge, yourself sitting perched on a stool high above the Vale of Evesham lazily sketching the magnificent view, you will have a mental picture of how I spent much of the week.

The evenings consisted of a similar mix of music and art – John and Sue talking about music and illustrating their subject practically; Moira and her husband Iain telling us how better to appreciate pictures, and again illustrating their talks with slides. The light relief was provided by John and the highlight of the week was when he demonstrated how to sing Strawberry Fair in five different voices, and how to set to music in six different styles a final demand from the Gas Board! The last evening, when there was a contribution from every member of the party, was a most memorable occasion.

And so it was goodbye to Dor Knap – but not before the friends made during the week had joined together in a celebration of Holy Communion, for our *raison d'etre* was always present. The sincere celebration in the simple chapel which is part of Dor Knap brought us all together better than any other act could have done. By the end of the week even the non-members had somehow become part of the family of Toc H.

We shall never again have the opportunity of visiting Dor Knap, with its quiet peace and its magnificent views; but the fellowship found there will, I know, be continued at the new acquisition of Toc H – The Bishop's House at Cuddesden. I know seven young people' who have an entirely new slant on Toc H. My own son has admitted to me that he never knew it would be like that; the seed has been sown, and here are potential future members of the age we're seeking.

The Conference Room looked out onto the Terrace, with its dry-stone walling, and was a popular focal point for artists

The Wardens

The roll of honour reads:

1959   Bill and Winifred Atkins
 (Bill died suddenly in the November)
1960   Charles and Kate Young
1961   George and Dorothy Atkinson
1962-1979   Tommy and Dorothy Trinder
Feb. to Dec. 1979 David and Clare Currant

Jean Taylor, until her untimely death, laid down the standards by her cooking and lived in the cottage that overlooked what later became the kitchen garden.

In at least one of the periods of interregnum Bob Purdy, a Yorkshire Area Secretary, 'held the fort'.

Charlie Young from Northumbria, with his fount of tales, and lovely Kate held the fort. Thereafter George would be remembered for his 'habit' of – out of the blue – sending typical Toc H postcards that simply said 'Thinking of you'.

George Atkinson a keen member from Melton Mowbray sold up his pork pie and butchers business and with his wife Dorothy brought an order, stability and commitment to the traditional movement.

The Wardens most remembered were Tommy and Dorothy Trinder who came from Barnet. They gave the house a wonderful informal buzz with lots of pranks and laughter to which their boys, when they were 'home', added as well. Big Alan, Michael, who went on to become a youth worker for 30 years, and Bobby 'the baby' who was very much part of the team that made their home our home.

There are many tales of Tommy and Dorothy's Wardenship and they certainly hosted and oversaw enormous developments, Tommy's gift of allocating the 'jobs' to every party with good-humoured banter is something everyone remembers.

Dorothy (*left*) in her own warm and inimitable style held sway in the kitchen and in all the domestic duties was ably assisted by a variety of casual staff who quickly seemed to pick up the sense of frivolity and fun that pervaded the house. The Trinder family made a rare and valued contribution to the house and Tommy has continued to live nearby in Broadway.

After Tommy's retirement in 1979 David and Clare Currant saw out the final days and oversaw the move to Cuddesdon, and they offer a Warden's perspective:

"We and our two boys were caught in the same spell as countless others when we attended our first Cotswold Festival (Dor Knap's last) in the summer of 1978 and, at the same time, assess the crazy notion that we might apply for the job of replacement wardens to Tommy and Dorothy. I had been in industry all my working life and Clare had secretarial and photographic experience, as well as being a capable mum and housewife. But we had little to qualify us for mass catering, managing a large property, organising very disparate types of bookings and working with groups of people who had come to learn more about themselves and this strange organisation called 'Toc H'. Neither of us were Toc H members, and our knowledge of the movement was confined to what we had been told by our lovely, enthusiastic next-door neighbour and "sponsor" Sue Cumming. However, this opportunity offered me a 'lifeline' from a career that had turned sour and for both of us a challenge that we believed we could meet. So we took "a leap in the dark" little knowing where it might lead. 1979 was a bigger challenge than either of us ever anticipated!

This is very much a Warden's perspective of Dor Knap, which we shared to a greater or lesser degree with those who came before us. The Wardens and their families experienced the same surroundings and atmosphere that have been described so vividly in these pages and a steady succession of that same rich company, but all within the framework of 'the job'. The job was hard graft: menus created, meals to be prepared – often for 30 or 40 (when Management Committees coincided with groups) – supplies to be purchased, laundry sent out, rooms cleaned, sticking plaster applied to maintenance jobs that required major surgery, groups welcomed, work parties organised, and somewhere along the line one's own family had to be cared for.

The Wardens' living quarters were also totally inadequate for a family of four and cramped for two: our bedroom just fitted a double bed wall to wall and the 'living room' was also the office and children's play room. However the major problem was the isolation. What?! With all those people trooping through the door every weekend and sometimes mid-week too, I hear you cry?! Yes, very interesting and very stimulating, but not the same as regular contact with local friends and neighbours and when you are doing a 7am to 11pm job in a rural setting there ain't time for all that! Our admiration for Tommy and Dorothy grew as the months went by; they were two in a million and Toc H owes them much.

Clare and I survived the Dor Knap experience for 11 months. There were many wonderful moments and some awful ones. We felt obliged to try and maintain the same level of service: something between a Youth Hostel and a Five Star hotel! Where else could you have had a daily fare of three cooked meals, morning coffee, afternoon tea and hot drinks and cakes before bed for the price that was paid in those days? The last mentioned evening drinks were a 'killer' requiring special stamina to summon energy and good humour during the evening hours.

Of course there were many compensations for all the hard slog. It was a very beautiful place to live, we enjoyed the wildlife, the walks, the sunrises and sunsets and the changing seasons that make the countryside such a joy. There were times of peace and freedom in between bookings and visits to local towns and villages. We made many new friends from amongst the staff and visitors, and were welcomed into the 'family' of Toc H.

It was a 'baptism by fire', but one which prepared us well for the move to Cuddesdon, though we never felt able to cut out the evening hot drinks and cakes!"

Clare & David Currant were the last Wardens of Dor Knap in 1979.

The Friends of Dor Knap

This section might well be subtitled 'The Nottinghamshire Connection' for, as **Frank Kirk** recalls, it was a weekend shared by the Notts. & Derbys and Beds, Herts. & North Bucks. areas in the very early 1960s that set the scene – the instigating force was some very uncomfortable beds and even more awful pillows.

The tales told by the men to their wives, and ladies known to them, about sleepless nights led to the womenfolk taking immediate action in making knitted toys, garments and cushions. One man ran a Post Office and apart from selling these extra articles, was able to buy some decent pillows from the millinery side of the shop. They then went with their car, stuffed full of pillows, back to Dor Knap and presented them to the house.

Some have also suggested that this was the first real breakthrough for women being seen to have a contribution to Dor Knap, for originally the then Warden, George Atkinson, insisted the house should be a 'male preserve'. Others recall that blanket making helped as well, and it was this type of activity that started the 'Friends of Dor Knap' with Frank and Dorothy Kirk becoming Chairman and Treasurer, and Mary Edwards from Bristol the Secretary.

This showed the potential of the 'the Friends' – on being asked what more they could do, the Chairman of Dor Knap Management Committee answered by asking if something couldn't be done about the kitchen!

Above: Members of the Wessex Pioneers: a young troupe who always gave memorable performances

Left: Decent pillows arrive, courtesy of Frank Kirk! Dorothy Trinder (left) with young Bobby and Tommy is on the right.

Only too happy to take on the challenge, Frank Kirk, who worked for (George) Wagstaffe and Appletons in Nottingham, told the story of Dor Knap to his boss. He suggested that Frank speak to the men in the engineering side who were able to help plan sizes, and so on, of a double drainer and superb suites which, with no payment to be made, sent Frank with these details to Pauls of Beeston. They were manufacturers of stainless steel kitchen equipment and organised that the equipment should be made and offered to Frank for Dor Knap – again without any payment, and even transported there free of charge as well!

Frank never forgot the kindness of his employers, which made the running of the kitchens so much more a pleasure than the antiquated equipment that had to suffice.

Another weekend memory that remains very clear is arriving with a group on a Friday evening, to be met by a group of over twenty enthusiastic young men and women, very scantily dressed in all manner of garments. This Toc H Mobile Action Group was called 'The Wessex Pioneers' from Dorset, and by the evening were ready to entertain; they appeared immaculately dressed, much to Frank's surprise, to gave a very memorable performance. The group decorated the area with flags, had 'sound' recording equipment, and were very professional. Apparently they often came to Dor Knap, arriving in up to six Bedford vans, which they had bought themselves, and living under canvas. At that time they were not members of Toc H – they just wanted to be a company of friends – until at least they were 21 years old.

Frank recalls stories about Phil Jacques from the Bingham Branch, who ran a small building firm with several employees also being Toc H members. They were some of the first volunteers of the 'Friends of Dor Knap' who, without charge, brought sand, cement and a will to work; they restored and rebuilt a great deal of the walls and rooms of Dor Knap to make them more habitable.

One of Dorothy Trinder's oft-told tales was when Arthur Fryman, a businessman and member from Nottingham, arrived at Dor Knap. He had a Rolls Royce that caused much amazement. Dorothy was heard to say that a parking space for such a vehicle should cost at least a fiver! Forever afterwards these extra parking fees were regularly paid to 'The Friends' as Arthur went to the house a great deal with his branch, his area, the Region, and the Central Executive. Arthur was in the Lace Trade originally as an engineer, and was extremely helpful in many ways, especially with purchasing new lawn mowers and then mowing the lawns at Dor Knap.

Not only was Dor Knap very special, but also many of the 'friends' who put all their time and devotion into the 'building up' of the Centre. Frank Kirk's employers must have had a very high regard for Toc H for they were also instrumental in providing the resources for the magnificent Toposcope, designed from a drawing by Jeff Christmas, that enabled us to put Dor Knap's wonderful vista in perspective. It stood on the front terrace on a plinth fitted by Martin Wenham and Frank himself.

Over the years The Friends of Dor Knap recruited many members and Branches to their number and they were able to purchase bedding, chairs, paint, brushes and a range of garden equipment and, not least, new cookers.

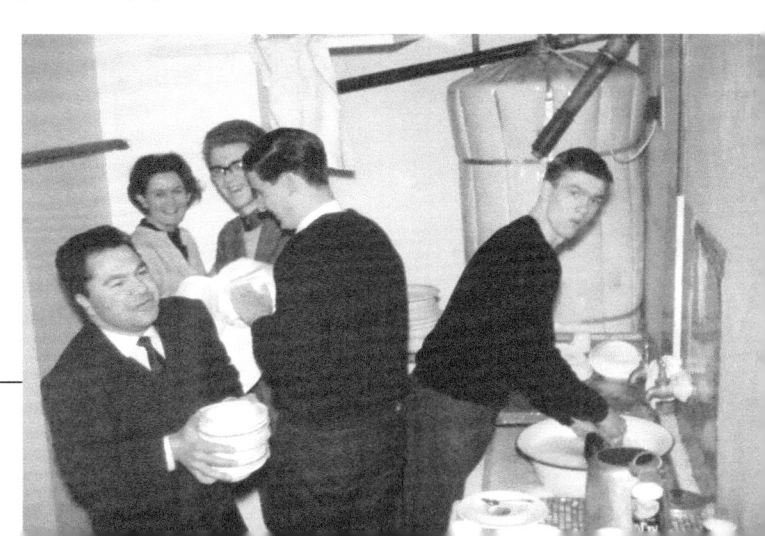

The old, antiquated kitchen facilities did nothing to dampen people's spirits!

The Cotswold Festivals

Most people are happy if, within their lifetime, they can see one of their dreams realised. John Callf had indeed seen this happen, and come to fruition with the establishment of Dor Knap as the Toc H Conference Centre. Then, through the success of the Music and Painting Weeks, he further dreamed of an amphitheatre in the grounds with a weekend of the Arts – and was eventually to serve on the very Committee that would see this dream realised.

Some may consider that the first attempt at such a Festival was rather 'amateurish' in both conception and employment, but so successful was the event, there was no hesitation in asking the same Committee to plan a successor. Future support and attendances however, proved the planning anything but amateurish with each successive Festival having a decisive ring of expertise about it.

From left: John Mitchell and George Lee, pictured here in 1972: two members of the Cotswold Festival Committee

At the outset, under the Chairmanship of the Rev. Bob Knight, the Committee consisted of the Rev. John Hull (as Artistic Director); George Lee (Secretary and Compere); Richard Ayshford-Sandford (Treasurer); John Callf; Sue Cumming (now the Rev. Sue Forshaw); Tommy Trinder (Warden); John Mitchell (in charge of car parking and organisation of daily work parties). Provision of refreshments was in the capable hands of Doug and Vera Ridgway and their family, supported by members of Walsall Branch, with security in the hands of Reg Wright and members of Broadway Branch.

One cannot look back on such Festivals without immediately recognising the mammoth task undertaken by some, particularly in catering not only for those actually participating in the weekend events, but also the hundreds of visitors daily from mid-morning to late evening. Nor should one underestimate the incredible task undertaken by John Mitchell and his gang in the very limited space above Dor Knap termed a 'car park' where daily they managed to squeeze a gallon into a pint pot yet still finding space for any latecomer.

To such 'heroes' must be added the names of Tommy and Dorothy Trinder who were forever busy in the house catering for the members of the committee and major demonstrators and exhibitors. Each Festival was opened with great gusto by a Silver Prize Band – initially by the Blockley Prize Band, succeeded by The Anstey Concert Band, The Walsall Metropolitan Band, and finally the Shipston Silver Prize Band, all of whom got their particular Festival off to a really rousing start. It was never difficult to maintain such a stirring tempo with a wide choice of musical tastes from a most colourful mixture of talented groups – the main support each day came from a group of singers gathered together and conducted by none other than John Hull.

These Singers formed the backbone of all the Festivals. They were a mixture of amateur and professional musicians who came together under the name of The New Anglian Singers, simply for the fun of it all. They were, first and foremost, a group of good friends. Other participating groups included Latchmere Junior School Steel Band in Battersea (an effort to encourage musical education among mixed races, bringing about a deeper understanding among people); The Tivoli Brass Ensemble (playing music of the Renaissance and Medieval periods); Martin and Christine Wenham (folk singing); The East Midlands Early Music Consort (a group of teacher friends from the East Midlands playing a variety of instruments); Peter Clayton and Chris Stern (who first met at a Dor Knap Folk Music weekend); Five in a Bar (in 1974 they had won the first ever Radio Two National Barber Shop Singing Contest – specialising in close harmony as well as authentic 'barber shop'); The Launton Handbell Ringers (who had appeared previously on both BBC Radio and TV and had given the first ever recital of handbell ringing in Coventry Cathedral). The Festivals also included The Latvian Dancers presenting valuable parts of Latvian culture with traditional songs and dances; The Gloucestershire Morris Men (a traditional feature of life in the Cotswolds and who better to demonstrate it than this particular group); The Bangladeshi Dance Group and many other musical and dance groups.

Always supporting the stage programme were a number of other events, including poetry reading held in the main conference room, in which Robin and Ann Gregory, Margaret and Brian Redding, Betty and Noel Cornick, Nancy Griffiths, and Ken Prideaux-Brune took part. At one such session those leading became aware that none other than Janet Suzman of the Royal Shakespeare Company was in their audience.

During each Festival a number of exhibitions and demonstrations were held on site to provide an even wider interest between the staged productions. These included Touchstone (Crispin and Mary White demonstrating their hobby of making exquisite jewellery from rocks and stones, and with it a study of geology); hand weaving (Jessica Rowley who had helped form the Wiltshire Guild of Spinners, Weavers and Dyers of which she had become its first Chairman); corn dollies (Marjorie Gibbard); stone carving and lettering (Martin Wenham) and many others ready to share their skills, interests and expertise.

Whilst the greater part of each Festival naturally took place in the open air the Games Room was always the focal point for a Art Exhibition. It was perhaps natural that the major part of each such exhibition came from those who normally supported the Annual Music and Painting Weeks held at Dor Knap, with John Davies, Ian Dawson, Cheryl Wood, Bob and Gwen Harvey, Moira Huntly, John Edwards, Reg Warters and Alan Coleman figuring prominently.

A photograph of a performance on the amphitheatre, c.1973

One traditional craft featuring was the making of Corn Dollies

The highlight one year was when regular contributors were joined by members of the Mouth and Foot Painters Association, including their Chairman Eric Stegmann with Elizabeth Twistington-Higgins MBE, Peter Spencer and Albert Baker. Eric had travelled especially from Germany for the occasion and to demonstrate in the course of that particular Festival. Elizabeth Twistington-Higgins (1923-1990) appeared not only as a highly skilled and internationally known artist, but also as the leader of The Chelmsford Dancers who had appeared several times on national TV, including 'Seeing and Believing' with John Hull and his Singers.

The dancer's spectacle of grace and charm had made them pioneers in the field of Liturgical Ballet. Elizabeth's attainment in the field of the Arts was outstanding in spite of total paralysis from polio in 1953 that cut short a blossoming ballet career. She overcame this disability to teach dancing and taught herself painting by mouth. Later she became a subject of *'This is Your Life'* and her book was a best-seller of its day.

For those that supported the Festivals however, best remembered will be the Dancers' performance, supported by John Hull and The Occasional Singers on the lawn at The Court, Broadway, the home of Richard Ayshford-Sandford a performance supported with items of poetry read by Ken Prideaux-Brune. The Dancers and Singers rounded off that special weekend with performances in Coventry Cathedral and the Old Church in Broadway (which stands opposite to the gateway leading up to Dor Knap).

Many members and friends will also remember it was through the encouragement of the Rev. Bob Knight that the Chelmsford Dancers later performed for Toc H in its Festival Service, held in Westminster Cathedral (RC), and in 1975 at a Festival Concert held in Westminster Central Hall.

Reflecting on so many happy and successful Festivals one cannot overlook the tremendous contribution made annually at the Festivals by the members of The Moseley and District Council of Churches Drama Group, under the able direction and leadership of John Bradley, who each Saturday evening performed a full version of a Shakespeare Play in the specially constructed amphitheatre.

The attraction of each performance was not only in the acting but the fact that Act 1 always commenced with natural lighting adding to the natural backdrop of Broadway and the Vale of Evesham; Act 2 saw stage lights being gradually introduced as dusk began to descend; and Act 3 was performed in pitch blackness with the stage fully floodlit and the twinkling lights of Broadway and Evesham providing a fairy-like backdrop until the final curtain.

A young group of singers, c.1970

One performance will be remembered above all others when, although the first Act went through in fairly fine weather, from the opening of Act 2 the weather definitely began to change as light rain began to fall. In the final Act the heavens really opened and the site became a wet and soggy mess with the lawn almost a mini-lake. As the rain fell, those on stage convinced that "the show must go on" and were supported by the sight of an audience determined to sit it out, come what may.

By the time of the final curtain it had turned into a heavy downpour with actors and audience alike thoroughly soaked. Those on stage stood to applaud the audience, whilst to a man the audience stood to applaud the cast equally enthusiastically. So much for Anthony and Cleopatra! It was indeed a memorable occasion and some members of the Committee, with Health and Safety in mind, still have nightmares as they recall the myriad of electrical cables wending across a sodden lawn to the stage and refreshment tent – we were greatly blessed that night in more ways than one, that is certain.

There is no doubt that one of the great joys of such Festivals was most of the performers, after making their own contribution, stayed on as part of the audience to support and encourage other participants. There was, as a result, a very relaxed and informal atmosphere, which all enjoyed, and that ensured each successive Festival became memorable, encouraged by a Committee which was itself equally relaxed; a group of friends working together for the sheer enjoyment of others.

After one Festival an exhibitor (a non-member of Toc H) wrote to the Festival Secretary, "I had no idea what I was letting myself in for but I found out that Toc H is a real experience and one has to be involved within its fellowship and its sincerity to understand and appreciate it. It was, for me, an unforgettable experience and one which I will treasure always as one of the happiest of my life".

Above and below: No Festival was complete without the traditional Morris Men.

One also remembers simple factors and individuals – such as Alec Churcher, a leading light in the early and formative years of Dor Knap, who during one Festival spent the whole Saturday morning just standing in the courtyard leaning on a broom, being prepared to chat with anyone and everyone who passed by. A timely reminder that a friendly welcome is just as important as any piece of practical work.

There was also one person, both a gifted musician and also a painter, who attended every annual Music and Painting Cotswold Festival. Jeff Christmas, an electrician by trade, had brought power to many of the outposts of Herefordshire and was one of many who contributed in no uncertain terms to the charm, the attraction and the history of Dor Knap.

Alec Churcher: Staff member and staunch supporter of the Cotswold Festival

A group at Warden's Week, with Jeff Christmas on the left who designed the Toposcope for the terrace and was heavily involved with the Cotswold Festival.

Cotswold Festivals of course did not just happen, for in addition to the required planning of each Festival much hard work was put into preparing the site and, in particular, the building of the amphitheatre and the tiered seating cut into the bank overlooking the stage. It was in this glorious spot at the final Festival in 1978, and with the Vale of Evesham as a backdrop in all its beauty, that a most memorable event took place. Knowing by then that the days of Toc H at Dor Knap were numbered, an open air Ecumenical Eucharist was held in the amphitheatre. It was a thanksgiving for all that Dor Knap had meant, not only to the Festivals but to all those who had, over some 20 years, discovered the fun shared and the friendships made, with the sheer joy of being together in the one place at this wonderful old house on the hill.

Dor Knap is now in private hands, but for so many within Toc H and its wider friendship, many happy memories will linger on in the hearts and minds, especially of those who in any measure joined in the Cotswold Festivals. Such memories: such bliss: such friends.

1939–1979: How this came to be written in 2004

When Margaret and Lionel Powell went to live in Stonehouse in Gloucestershire they discovered one of their neighbours, 87 year old Priscilla Joseph, was writing her family memoirs and as she had lived in 'Dor Nap' (she insists on that spelling!) and realised the Toc H connection, she suggested they might be allies in obtaining further memories – in particular photographs of the house since her family left at the end of the second World War.

In the Summer of 2003, Lionel wrote to *Point Three*, the Toc H Journal, and an article appeared in the September issue that year asking for any information, reminiscences or photographs to be sent to him. The response was enormous and before long it became apparent that there was enough material forthcoming to make a significant publication to mark the Toc H life of Dor Knap between 1959-1979. One of those to respond was Ray Fabes who had spent 15 years on the Toc H staff (1959-1974) and was a very frequent participant in Dor Knap ventures. During his last year on the staff in the East Midlands Region he recruited Lionel Powell from West Pinchbeck Branch in Lincolnshire to come on a project in Peterborough.

From that experience Lionel changed his life's direction and ultimately worked for the Langley House Trust before finally settling in Stonehouse in Gloucestershire. George Lee was another who responded and, well, George seems to have been around in Toc H forever! He was Area Secretary in the West Midlands and therefore the local staff man in the Region. George's particular contribution as a co-author of this publication – as well as writing two key sections – has been checking all the fine details from the accounts and records that were sent to us, and suggesting (with others) further people who might be encouraged to offer their perspectives.

Various other people who had played a part in the development of the house were contacted, and again the response was immediate, finishing with over 50 people writing pieces for us and sending photographs.

Lionel Powell (left) and Ray Fabes in 2004

An Enduring Friendship

George Lee and Tommy Trinder first met each other at Dor Knap in the early 1960s and are still good friends some forty years on.

In the photos (*below*) the top one was probably taken in the mid-1960s and apparently they were watching a work party depart for a days work.

The second photo was taken in Broadway, 2004, where Tommy (in his nineties) still lives today. At regular intervals, George meets with him for a lunchtime pint and a chat about the 'good old days'.

A Towering Photo

Finally, we loved this picture but did not have room to place it anywhere else: a photo of John Burgess, c.1960, doing a giant act on Broadway Tower!

John was an active member of staff at Toc H for over forty years before retiring in 2003.

Postscript: Dor Knap today

John Mitchell writes; "After Toc H's time at Dor Knap, the house was sold off as part of the general sale of the Middle Hill estate by Lord Dulverton's youngest son.

In due course Dor Knap became, and still is, a private family home. The estate agent's magnificent brochure of 1999 (*see picture below*) Illustrates a sumptuous residence set in 190 acres of fields and woodland. The asking price was by today's standards, a relatively modest £1.75 million.

During the 1990s major extensions and alterations were carried out. Little now remains of the house that Toc H members knew and loved, apart from the conference room (now with more windows and French doors out to the garden) and the inglenook fireplace in what used to be the 'Snug'. What used to look like a cosy farmhouse is now a very up-market, elegant country house (albeit from the same mellow Cotswold stone).

A second storey has also been built throughout – and one can only imagine the wonderful views from the bedroom built above the old conference room. A leisure complex and indoor swimming pool was built behind the old 'Snug'. The house itself was extended further up the hill and a range of stables was added. A paddock for horses was created and the old yew trees, including the 'Teapot', were all removed to make it 'horse friendly'.

The drive has been discontinued, and is now grassed at the top, and access is via the road that turns up beside Middle Hill house... but the land still falls away to the North East, the stunning views remain, the rooks still call out from the stands of trees higher up the hill, and the old wrought iron sign that used to hang by the chapel (see photograph on front cover) was finally returned in 2004."

Dor Knap in 1999. The house had already undergone dramatic changes during new ownership. Note the second storey to the old Conference Room and the disappearance of the Chapel.

Photo courtesy Strutt & Parker and Knight Frank Intl.

Appendix I: What is Toc H?

Or, as someone once asked recently after seeing the logo on a member's shirt, "What is 'Tosh'...?"

Toc H is a movement of the 20th century. It grew out of the horrors of the First World War, and its early momentum came from a desire to do all that could be done to avoid a repetition of that suffering. Over the years its work has changed as it responded to changes in society. But the ideals with which it began remain.

Where it all started back in 1915: Talbot House in Poperinghe, Belgium.

In 1915, an army chaplain called Rev. Philip Thomas Byard 'Tubby' Clayton (1885-1972) opened a soldiers' club in a house in Poperinge, behind the allied lines in Belgium. The house had a remarkable atmosphere – men of different ranks were encouraged to mingle and make friends, ignoring all the normal rules of rank – the sign inside reads; "All rank abandon, ye who enter here".

At the top of the house an attic, which had formerly been a hop loft, became an 'Upper Room' chapel. Those who used the house were young men facing imminent death and many found unlikely but close friendships. Many also found spiritual help. The house was called Talbot House after Lieut. Gilbert Talbot, a son of the Bishop of Winchester, who had been killed near Ypres. The soldiers affectionately called the house by its initials, 'Toc' being the signallers' code for the letter 'T' and the Movement that formed after the war called itself by this nickname.

In 1929 Lord Wakefield presented the 'Old House' to Toc H through an Anglo-Belgian Association, and partially endowed it. Talbot House is now a focus for pilgrims to the Flanders Fields as well as a centre for reconciliation and the Movement's continuing involvement with the Belgian community.

Early in 1920, many of the men who had found something special in Talbot House decided that this should not be lost. They established a house in central London where young men on their own in the capital could find a place to lodge, a group of companions and an opportunity to work in the local community.

Before long, there were many more such houses and later, other outlets sprang up around the country in the form of local branches – these were founded on the ideals of fellowship and local service.

A very early photo of Rev. P. B. 'Tubby' Clayton, Toc H founder, pictured c.1920

The Lamp and its significance

Part of the service still practised at any Toc H gathering is the lighting of the Lamp followed by the reading of the 4th verse from *'For The Fallen'* (*see below*) written in 1914 by Laurence Binyon (1869-1943).

Shown here is a typical lamp used by the Women's Association; a superb bronze casting mounted on a wood base.

In 1922, the League of Women Helpers of Toc H was formed. The original members were nurses who had used Talbot House (one of them being the Founder Pilot, Alison McFie) and numerous others who had been associated with the House through relatives and friends. In 1943, the LWH was renamed Toc H (Women's Section) and, in 1952, Toc H Women's Association. The two organisations were integrated in 1971.

When Toc H members travelled and settled abroad between the wars, they took Toc H with them. There are now a number of autonomous, but very closely linked organisations, all over the world.

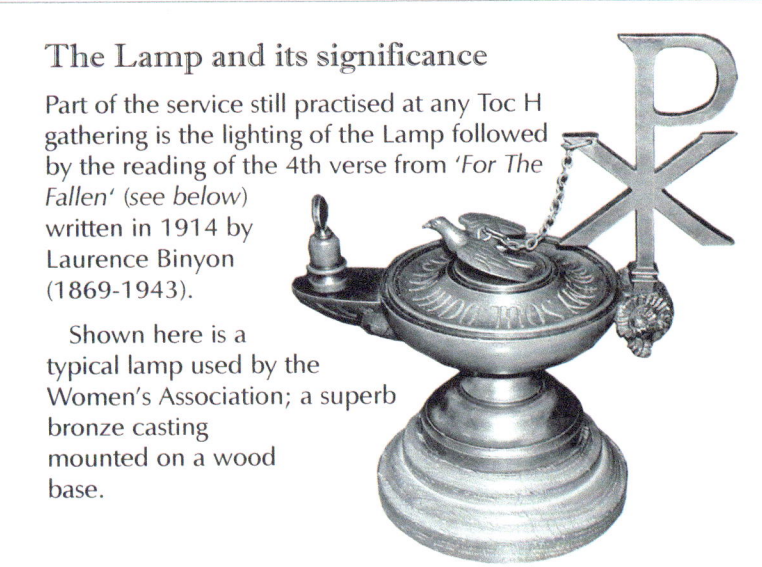

We will remember them…

They shall not grow old, as we that are left grow old,

Age shall not weary them, nor the years condemn.

At the going down of the sun and in the morning,

We will remember them.

Appendix II: Artwork

Many excellent drawings and painting must have been produced during Toc H's tenure. In particular, the reader is drawn towards the drawing by John Davies and the following pen and ink art created by Gary Jones.

All drawings on this page are printed with permission and are copyright © Gary Jones

Appendix III: Domesday Book

The Domesday Book (*below*) was an incredible feat: instigated by William I in 1085, within two years every single plot of land had been painstakingly catalogued and valued.

Broadway's entry translates from the original Norman text as follows:

> *The church itself holds BROADWAY. There are 30 hides paying geld. In demesne are 3 ploughs; and a priest and 42 villans with 20 ploughs. There are 8 slaves. The whole TRE was worth £12.10s: now £14.10s.*

Broadway was originally named 'Bradeweia' and the term 'TRE' (Tempore Regis Edwardi) is used to value a possession from the time of King Edward I.

'Geld' referred to a tax based on the 'hide', which was a notional amount based on the land required to support a family. 'Demesne' meant the produce from the lands was owned by the Lord. A 'villan' was not a 'villain' (as in outlaw) but simply meant a villager.

For those younger readers, £14.10s is £14.50—imagine, the whole village could be bought for the price of a CD!

Appendix IV: Changing logos

The Toc H logo has undergone many transitions. During the earlier part of Dor Knap occupation, the first logo was used. Sometime in the mid-1960s the radically different 'world' logo was introduced. Lastly, the current logo came about well after Toc H left Dor Knap.

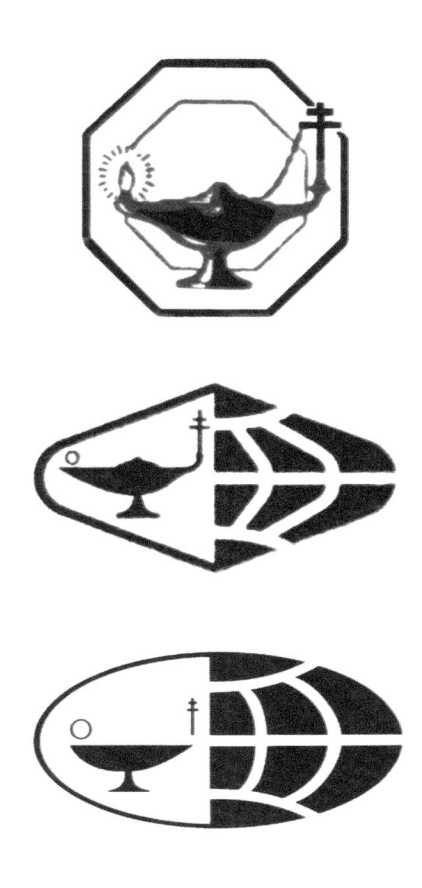

Acknowledgements

Although in our introduction we suggested it would be invidious to name particular individuals who had contributed significantly to this publication, we did ultimately decide to identify some by name in the text and further to those acknowledgements we would like to place on record our grateful thanks to John Burgess for an archive of Dor Knap material, and to Marcya Lennox of the Birmingham Evening Post who negotiated with Agents who were selling the Estate and secured us a copy of their brochure – all because Nora Warner's sharp eyes spotted the advertisement.

Special thanks to all our "peer reviewers" who recommended several changes of emphasis in our final draft. Lastly, but by no means least, a special tribute to Priscilla Joseph for without her initial question none of this would have been written and we include her contribution "Dor Nap before Toc H". It seems fitting to come that full circle in conclusion. Additionally to:

Ken Prideaux-Brune & John Mitchell, for scrutiny, encouragement and memories.

David Hardy, for advice on the editing of photographs and the use of scanning equipment.

Shelia Avery, for invaluable help while researching the history of Dor Knap, its owners and residents.

Dr Robert Bearman, Head of Archives and Local Studies, Records Office, Shakespeare Birthplace Trust

References

Noake's Guide to Worcestershire: John Noake, 1868

Toc H Conference and Training Centre (booklet): Alec Churcher, 1959

The Song of Dor Knap: John Callf, Sunday Mercury, 1967

Cotswold Landscapes: Rob Talbot and Robin Whiteman, © 1999

www.campdenwonder.plus.com - 'The Campden Wonder': © Peter Clifford, 2004

Domesday Book, A Complete Translation: Penguin Books, © 1992

Index

A
Alison House **19**, 41
Art & Crafts Movement 11
Atkins, Bill and Winifred 44
Atkinson, Dorothy 33, 44
Atkinson, George 25, 44, 46
Ayshford-Sandford, Richard 16, 18, 36, 48, 50

B
Barker, Ivor 25
Batsford Park 16
Benedictine Abbey 9
Bordon Company 26, 30, 35
Bothy 18, 21, 23, 32, 40
Bowler, Keith 26
Bradley, John 51
Broadway, Hill & Tower 5, 7, **9-13**, 15, 16, 20, 23-25, 31, 33-35, 38, 42, 44, 48, 50, 51, 54, 59
Burgess, John 25, 26, 54, 60
Burne-Jones, Edward 11

C
Callf, John 12, 16-18, 26, 30, 35, 41, 48, 60
Campden Wonder, The 10, 60
Cattell, Cyril 27, 30
Chapel, The 5, 18, 21, 23, 26, **28-30**, 39
Christmas, Jeff 47, 52
Church Street 10
Churcher, Alec 12, 18, 26, 30, 40, 52, 60
Civil War 9
Clayton Volunteer 19, 28, 41
Clayton, Tubby, Rev. P B 20, 26, 30, 34, 56
Clumps 28, 33
Conference Room 18, 20, 22, 36, 39
Conwy/Conway 38, 39
Cotswolds 5, 9-12, 16, 24, 26, 27, 32, 42, 48, 49, 55, 60
Cotswold Festival 23, 44, **48-52**
Coventry Cathedral 49, 50
Cromack, Harry 30
Crown and Trumpet, The 21, 34
Cuddesdon House 18, 19, 41, 43-45
Cumming, Sue 27, 31, 42, 44, 48
Currant, Clare & David 19, 44

D
Davies, Col. John 27, 35, 36, 49, 58
Dawson, Ian 36, 49
Domesday Book 5, 9, 12, 59, **60**
Dulverton, Lord, of Batford 13, 16-18, 20, 42, 55
Dyrham, Battle of 9

E
Edwards, Mary 30, 46

F
Fabes, Ray 30, 31, 53
Ferrier, Kathleen 33
Fish Hill 10
Flower, Edgar 13
Friends of Dor Knap 5, 30, **46, 47**
Fryman, Arthur 47

G
Games Room 23, 28, 39, 49
Griffiths, Cec. 42

H
Halliwell(-Phillipps), James 13
Harvey, Gwyn 35
High Street 10
Hull, Rev. John 18, 27, 32, 34, 36, 37, 42, 48, 50
Huntly, Moira 36, 42, 43, 49

I
Inglenook 12, 32, 40, 55

J
Jacques, Phil 23, 47
Jones, Gary 58
Joseph, Priscilla 14, 53, 60

K
Kirk, Frank 46, 47
Knight, Margery 22, 24, 29, 37
Knight, Rev. Bob 29, 48, 50

L
Lee, George 19, 48, 53, 54
Llanarmon-yn-Iâl 36, 38
Llwynegrin Singers 37
Lygon Arms 9

M
McFie, Alison 19, 57
Malvern Hills 41
Malverns 12
Mead, Richard 15
Middle Hill 5, 11, **12-14**, 16, 18, 23, 55
Middle Hill Press 11
Mitchell, Jennifer (nee Lythgoe) 19
Mitchell, John 33, 40, 48, 55, 60
Morris, William 11, 49

N
Night Exercises 24

P
Painting and Music Week 5, 27, 32, 36, 37, **42**
Phillipps, Sir Thomas 11, 13
Poperinge 19, 26, 56
Powell, Lionel 53
Prideaux-Brune, Ken 19, 31, 41, 49, 50, 60
Prideaux-Brune, Lance 20

R
Ranagazoo 28, 30, 32, 33
Reformation 9
Ridgway, Doug and Vera 48
Rossetti, Dante Gabriel 11
Rudd, Colin 25

S
Schools Week 31
Shakespeare 49, 51, 60
Smith, Bertha 40
Smith, Rev. Ron 33
Snowshill 10, 15, 16, 23, 24, 35

Snug 18, 20, 32, 40, 55
St. Eadburgha 9, 10
Stratford-upon-Avon 13, 24, 25
Strathman, Bob 21
Suzman, Janet 49

T
Talbot House 19, 26, 30, 56, 57
Talbot, Gilbert 56
Taylor, Jean 19, 44
Teapot, The 22, 55
Television 26
The Green 10
This Is Your Life 26, 50
Thompson, Robert, "Mouse Man" 20
Till, Dennis 25
Toposcope 21, 47
Trinder, Dorothy 32, 44, 47, 48
Trinder, Tommy 24, 26, 32, 40, 48, 54
Tryfan 20
Turner, Pat and Jack 25
Twistington-Higgins, Elizabeth 50

V
Vale of Evesham 12, 21, 24, 35, 39, 41, 43, 51, 52

W
Wagstaffe and Appletons 21, 46
Wakefield, David 33
Warden Manor 19, 30
Warden's Weeks 26
Warmington, 'Warmy' 21
Wesley, John 10
Wessex Pioneers, The 47
Wills, family 13, 16
Window Tax 12
World Chain of Light 26, 30
Wright, Reg 48

Y
Young, Charles and Kate 44